HIS WORLD NEVER DIES:
THE EVOLUTION OF JAMES BOND

Dave Holcomb

JAMES BOND CHEAT SHEET

Movie	Actor Playing Bond	Release Year
Dr. No	Sean Connery	1962
From Russia with Love	Sean Connery	1963
Goldfinger	Sean Connery	1964
Thunderball	Sean Connery	1965
You Only Live Twice	Sean Connery	1967
On Her Majesty's Secret Service	George Lazenby	1969
Diamonds Are Forever	Sean Connery	1971
Live and Let Die	Roger Moore	1973
The Man with the Golden Gun	Roger Moore	1974
The Spy Who Loved Me	Roger Moore	1977
Moonraker	Roger Moore	1979
For Your Eyes Only	Roger Moore	1981
Octopussy	Roger Moore	1983
A View to a Kill	Roger Moore	1985
The Living Daylights	Timothy Dalton	1987
License to Kill	Timothy Dalton	1989
Goldeneye	Pierce Brosnan	1995
Tomorrow Never Dies	Pierce Brosnan	1997
The World is Not Enough	Pierce Brosnan	1999
Die Another Day	Pierce Brosnan	2002
Casino Royale	Daniel Craig	2006
Quantum of Solace	Daniel Craig	2008
Skyfall	Daniel Craig	2012
Spectre	Daniel Craig	2015

FREE GIFT

As a thank you for purchasing my book, I would like to offer readers more cheat sheets to help them with the history of the Bond series as they read. For additional cheat sheets on Bond girls, villains, and songs, check out the link below:

http://www.rebrand.ly/hisworldneverdiesfreegift

To Ewok,

Who needs a Bond girl when I have you?

"I've spent a lifetime running
And I always get away
But with you I'm feeling something
That makes me want to stay...

...If I risk it all
Could you break my fall?

How do I live? How do I breathe?
When you're not here I'm suffocating
I want to feel love, run through my blood
Tell me is this where I give it all up?
For you I have to risk it all
'Cause the writing's on the wall."[1]

- Sam Smith, "Writing's on the Wall" from *Spectre* (2015)

---

[1] Smith, Sam. "Writing's On The Wall." Capitol Records. B002410421, 2015, compact disc.

TABLE OF CONTENTS

FOREWORD

At times, this book will cover topics some readers may find sensitive, such as femininity, masculinity, homosexuality and racism in western society and how it pertains to the James Bond film series.

For the purposes of these discussions, the author did his best to ensure every word and phrase was factually and politically correct to the best of his knowledge. If anyone takes any issue with a specific word choice or phrase, feel free to reach out to the author. He is more than willing to listen to new perspectives.

Specifically, Holcomb thoroughly deliberated how or whether to use the terms "black people" and/or "African American" in this book. In journalism school, he learned the best thing to do for a story in which race was relevant was to ask the individual his or her preference. However, that's not possible in a situation where fictional characters and countries are being discussed.

Upon the advice of The National Association of Black Journalists, Holcomb decided to use "black" and "black people" during race analysis in this book. "African American" was used in situations where the author was able to 100 percent confirm that the person of discussion identified himself as both American and from African descent. The NABJ also advises that black and white should not be capitalized; that style was used throughout this text.[2]

For clarity, the author also chose to use the term "Bond girls" despite the fact some feminists may find the term offensive. Holcomb respects that ideology, but to avoid confusion, "Bond girls" and not "Bond women" was used upon nearly every reference.

---

[2] "African American, African-American, Black, black," *The Diversity Style Guide*, April 13, 2019, https://www.diversitystyleguide.com/glossary/african-american-african-american-black-2/.

INTRODUCTION

As kids, my sister always had an easier time falling asleep. One fateful vacation night, that worked to my benefit.

Unable to sleep in my family's hotel room, I was allowed to watch television with my parents. They found *The World is Not Enough* (1999), and thus, I received my first introduction to James Bond.

I was about 11 years old at the time. My dad eventually went to bed, but my mom and I finished the movie at about midnight. Back in the day, *Spike TV* turned a two-hour movie into a three-hour event, but the next day, our family did spend time discussing the series and what made this film great.

Then when I was 12, I saw *Die Another Day* (2002) on a Saturday in December with my dad, and best friend, Jake. More specifically, it was Dec. 14, 2002. I know this because I still have the ticket stub.

Over the years, I've kept a lot of ticket stubs, but the ticket to my first Bond adventure in theaters is one of the oldest in my collection. Obviously, the film left an impression on me.

Figure 1: Fun fact - a matinee movie ticket in 2002 cost $4.75

Action movies have always been my favorite, starting with Indiana Jones and Star Wars. I remember once when I was six, I decided I wanted to watch all three episodes of the original Star Wars trilogy on the same day. I made it through *Star Wars* (1977), but before starting *The Empire Strikes Back* (1980), my mom said we had to leave the house to run errands.

I unfortunately didn't get through the trilogy that day. But I certainly did the following day, restarting from the beginning and working my way through all 376 minutes of the three films.

On Dec. 14, 2002, James Bond didn't surpass either Star Wars or Indiana Jones as my favorite action series, but *Die Another Day* was, by far, the coolest thing I'd ever watched. It had everything an action movie needed from the invisible car to the music.

I hummed that theme song for days.

My Bond fandom really took off the following Christmas when I discovered several TV tape recordings of 007 movies. One night, my dad and I randomly chose to watch *Moonraker* (1979). I remember also watching *You Only Live Twice* (1967) for the first time. It was the same day Carson Palmer won the Heisman Trophy (did I mention I'm a huge sports fan too?).

We watched both in my room, and my sister joined too while she wrapped Christmas gifts. It was our last family Christmas in our hometown of Pittsburgh before we moved to New Jersey the following summer.

From then on, I couldn't get enough Bond, and the best part about it was, with more than 20 films, you can't possibly watch them all in one day.

I did slowly work through the family VHS Bond tapes. Then on Christmas day, my dad received the 007 Special Edition: Volume 1 DVD set, which included *Dr. No* (1962), *Goldfinger* (1964), *The Man with the Golden Gun* (1974), *The Spy Who Loved Me* (1977), *License to Kill* (1989), *Goldeneye* (1995), and *Tomorrow Never Dies* (1997).

I'd have to look up what movies were in the second and third sets, but that first one is hard to forget.

By the time the series released *Casino Royale* (2006) three years later, I had probably seen all the previous films at least twice. In many cases, much more than that, and like every great Bond fan, I had my own series ranking from the best film to the worst.

When I saw *Casino Royale*, I thought I was going to know exactly how the film would progress. There would be a cool action sequence at the beginning followed by the opening credits and song. Then, the film would dive into the plot, where some evil mastermind wanted to do something terrible, Q would help by providing some great gadgets, Bond would meet some attractive women and then save the world.

Casino Royale possessed most of these elements but constructed them differently, and I couldn't understand why. The change didn't go over so well with me, as I basically hated the new direction. Why on earth would anyone mess with the Bond formula?

Regardless, I watched it at Christmastime every year during high school because that's when I watched every Bond film. My high school friend, George, and I made this a tradition.

Upon re-watching *Casino Royale* as a freshman in college, I enjoyed it a lot more. After suffering my first broken heart that year, I easily connected with Bond's heartache after Vesper Lynd's betrayal.

For the first time, I related to Bond in reality and not just in fantasy.

Three years later, *Skyfall* (2012) hit theaters during the Christmas season. Afterwards, I finally began to understand why the series made the drastic change in direction in 2006. Since coming to this realization, the Craig era as Bond has become a lot more likable.

In this book, I'd like to pass along my theories as to why change was necessary for the series, and how it has prosperously executed the change. Please note that this book will include analysis of only the films (not the novels) and don't worry, Bond movie rankings will not be found in the following pages.

The truth is, there is no perfect 007 film. There isn't one formula anymore. Some are a lot better than others, but each film has at least one redeeming aspect. Such lists are subjective anyway -- harboring even more opinion than ranking the best Super Bowl teams of all time (did I also mention I went to school for sports journalism?).

Just like football, Bond has been forced to adapt with culture and society. But the series is alive and well because those changes have been largely successful.

Over the decades, the Bond film series has evolved its portrayal of masculinity, femininity, sexuality and race. Music, the power of nostalgia and fan theories have helped keep Bond current and popular as well, and we're about to dive into it all and more.

1

FRAGILE MODERN MASCULINITY

He arrived on screen long ahead of other action heroes such as Wolverine, Jason Bourne and Ethan Hunt. Before even Indiana Jones, John McClane or Han Solo debuted, there was one hero in the action genre by the name of "Bond .... James Bond."[3]

As the longest-running movie series in American film history, 007 set the standard for the action genre in the early 1960's. Ever since, all action heroes have been compared to him.

In his debut scene during *Dr. No*, the audience learns the quintessential aspects of the Bond character and the series -- he's the ultimate action hero. His masculinity is transcendent, as he's the coolest cat around and virtually irresistible to every woman he meets.

Sylvia Trench (Eunice Gayson), who appears on screen before 007, becomes the very first Bond girl. Trench and Bond meet at the baccarat table, which is his game of choice in the casinos. He rarely loses -- that is, at both winning a hand and the girl.

---

[3] *Dr. No*. Directed by Terence Young. 1962. Beverly Hills, CA: United Artists, DVD.

The composure in which Sean Connery portrays Bond in this first scene has rarely been duplicated through the series. It certainly has never been surpassed. Perhaps unknown to a modern-day audience, Bond is playing Chemin de fer, which is strictly a game of chance.

The fact Bond wins several hands in a row showcases his good fortune. This works to foreshadow all the luck he will possess throughout the series -- narrowly escaping death and saving the world from major destruction time and time again -- but the biggest takeaway is Bond's mannerisms. Even when things are out of his control, he never flinches -- not in the casino nor in his profession.

In other words, he personifies the epitome of what is considered masculine in the early 1960's. Connery's Bond is about as tough as they come, and yet, he's smirky, smiling in the face of that game of chance -- or a beautiful woman.

"In the 1960's, Connery portrayed Bond as charismatic machismo," Irish journalist Craig Cunningham wrote in 2013. "A man's man of the time, a hairy chested, heavy drinking, constantly smoking representation of the everyday man."[4]

The only thing more obvious than Bond's love of women is the women's affection for him. Trench follows Bond out of the casino when he abruptly leaves because duty calls. When Bond asks her to a golf-dinner date, she tries to act uninterested, and yet, a few scenes later, Bond discovers she has broken into his

---

[4] Craig Cunningham, "James Bond: A character of masculinity," *Sport, Music, Economics, Politics, Media,* April 21, 2013, https://craigcc11.wordpress.com/2013/04/21/james-bond-a-character-of-masculinity/.

apartment with the intent to seduce him. Trench accomplishes this by wearing one of Bond's dress shirts -- and nothing else.

> Trench: [while playing miniature golf in Bond's apartment wearing only his dress shirt] I decided to accept your invitation.

> Bond: [holstering his gun] That was for tomorrow afternoon. Tell me, do you always dress this way for golf?

> Trench: I changed into something more comfortable. Oh, I hope I did the right thing.

> Bond: You did the right thing, but you picked the wrong moment. I have to leave immediately.

> Trench: Oh, that's too bad. [moves closer to Bond] Just as things were getting interesting again. [They kiss] When did you say you have to leave?

> Bond: Immediately. [They kiss again] Almost immediately.[5]

Trench is hardly the only woman to fall head over heels for Bond in *Dr. No*. The British spy kicks off his movie series sleeping with three different women. When Bond retrieves his room key at a Jamaican hotel, even the female hotel clerk can't help but stare at Bond as he walks past, perhaps fantasizing about what it might be like to see him without his perfectly tailored suit.

This is repeated with multiple female hotel desk clerks throughout the 1960's. It helps convey that Bond is irresistible.

---

[5] *Dr. No.* 1962.

Throughout the series, women rarely reject Bond, as he wins over whichever woman he desires or needs in order to achieve world peace. This is the best way in which the film writers and creators develop the idea that Bond is the perfect man. Men want to take on some portion of his personality while women just plain want him.

But in order to remain popular and relevant, the series and Bond character have undergone alterations. The evolution of masculinity in the series has somewhat occurred seamlessly with the insertion of each new actor as 007.

In addition to toughness, Connery portrays Bond with a ruggedness that wasn't matched again until Craig in 2006. He's rough around the edges, but Connery's 007 is also smirky and witty, which helps make him a more likeable character.

If he has any weaknesses, it is not apparent to the 1960's audience. That's exactly how boys from the Silent and Baby Boomer generations (the original Bond could be from either) were taught to act -- rarely show emotion or affection and, as Q stated in *The World is Not Enough*, "never let anyone see you bleed."[6]

In the late 1960's, George Lazenby brought more stylish and physical aspects to the character and series. *On Her Majesty's Secret Service* (1969) showcased the most complex action sequences to date, and Lazenby carried himself with a bit more sophistication as opposed to Connery's abruptness.

---

[6] *The World is Not Enough*. Directed by Michael Apted. 1999. Beverly Hills, CA: MGM/United International Pictures, DVD.

By the end of *On Her Majesty's Secret Service*, the Bond character goes in an entirely new direction. He marries Tracy di Vicenzo (Diana Rigg) in what was originally an arranged marriage, but both Bond and di Vicenzo fall in love.

Unfortunately for Bond, differing greatly from the rest of the series, this film doesn't end happily. Bond's arch nemesis, Ernst Stavro Blofeld (Telly Savalas) drives by the lover's marriage coach (their car) parked on the side of the road and kills di Vicenzo in a barrage of gunfire.

This leaves the audience heartbroken. Bond is holding his dead wife in his arms on their wedding day, whispering their favorite saying "We have all the time in the world."[7] That phrase is repeated throughout the film and is the inspiration for Louis Armstrong's song featured in the film, which is also called "We Have All the Time in the World." It becomes a major theme to the movie, as di Vicenzo's death demonstrates human life never really lasts as long as one would like.

Yet still, Bond's face remains mostly emotionless. Originally, Lazenby performed this final scene with a few tears running down his face, but director Peter Hunt told him to do the scene again without crying.[8]

---

[7] *On Her Majesty's Secret Service*. Directed by Peter Hunt. 1969. Beverly Hills, CA: United Artists, DVD.
[8] George Simpson, "'James Bond DOESN'T cry' George Lazenby wasn't allowed tears for 007's dead wife," Express, August 8, 2017, https://www.express.co.uk/entertainment/films/838644/James-Bond-wife-death-George-Lazenby-Diana-Rigg-On-Her-Majesty-s-Secret-Service.

Despite a lost marriage and broken heart, Bond shows little emotion. Because at the time, that's what the ultimate man would do.

Following a brief return of Connery, Roger Moore stepped into the 007 role for the 1970's and early 1980's. His portrayal of the character featured less toughness and more wit. Moore's Bond had the most comedic lines, which were often cheesy.

During this era, the series featured extra fun -- compared to the 1960's films -- and reflected the more relaxed times in America, as the country moved away from the Red Scare and Vietnam. Moore showcased a cleaner image and boyish charm, perhaps indicating that men at that time didn't have to be so cold and emotionless. Still, Bond didn't display many feelings during this era either.

The best examples of this come during *The Spy Who Loved Me*. Upon meeting Major Anya Amasova (Barbara Bach), who is Russian Agent XXX, Bond and Amasova showcase their "spying" abilities by revealing what they know about each other. For the first time since 1969, this scene references Bond's marriage.

Amasova: Commander James Bond, recruited to the British Secret Service from the Royal Navy. License to kill and has done so on numerous occasions. Many lady friends but married only once. Wife killed ...

Bond: [interrupting] Alright, you've made your point.

Amasova: You're sensitive, Mr. Bond.

Bond: About some things, yes.[9]

By the late 1970's, the Bond series was finally ready to admit that its hero could be sensitive, but he's hardly delicate. While he concedes to having emotions, 007 still doesn't show them, instead changing the subject rather quickly. This idea has the Bond character closer to its modern-day version, but still he expresses a stony personality. At this point, it was acceptable for men to have feelings, but not openly.

That's the extent of Bond admitting to any feelings. In another exchange with Amasova, Bond is rather apathetic when he discovers he has killed her lover.

> Amasova: The man I loved. He was in Berngarten (Austria) three weeks ago. Did you kill him?
>
> Bond: When someone's behind you on skis at 40 miles per hour trying to put a bullet in your back, you don't always have time to remember a face. In our business, Anya, people get killed. We both know that. So did he. It was either him or me. The answer to the question is yes. I did kill him.
>
> Amasova: Then, when this mission is over, I will kill you.[10]

Bond's forthrightness and honesty are commendable, but without an official apology, it's a rather callous answer. His response to her question is only one step better than, "Yep, I killed him. Deal with it." But in 1977, this answer exemplifies

---

[9] *The Spy Who Loved Me.* Directed by Lewis Gilbert. 1977. Beverly Hills, CA: MGM/United Artists, DVD.
[10] *The Spy Who Loved Me.* 1977.

how a man was probably supposed to answer a tough question -- truthfully and to the point.

If Amasova asked Timothy Dalton's Bond the same question 10 years later, she might not have received the same heartless response. By 1987 when Dalton becomes Bond, sensitivity in men and their ability to show vulnerability have increased, and it's reflected in the Bond character. Dalton's 007 grows more attached to the women he sleeps with, and he appears to have a stronger interest in their well-being.

New York Times journalist Barbara Ehrenreich wrote about this new development in masculinity in 1984:

> I see the change in the popular images that define masculinity, and I see it in the men I know, mostly in their 30's, who are conscious of possessing a sensibility and even a way of life that is radically different from that of their fathers. These men have been, in a word, feminized, but without necessarily becoming more feminist. In fact, I do not think that those of us who are feminists either can or, for the most part, would want to take credit for the change.[11]

In *The Living Daylights* (1987), Bond lies to Kara Milovy (Maryam d'Abo), the Bond girl of the film, about his relationship with villain General Georgi Koskov (Jeroen Krabbé) in order to gain intel on the defected Russian general. But 007 and Milovy have an obvious connection. After traveling together for several days, Bond attempts to come clean with his lie before engaging in anything beyond kissing. Twenty-two

---

[11] Ehrenreich, Barbara. "A Feminists' View of the New Man," *The New York Times*, May 20, 1984.

years earlier in *Thunderball* (1965), Connery's Bond didn't admit the full truth with Domino (Claudine Auger) until after they had already had sex, which gave 007 an extra advantage in his cold manipulation.

Dalton combines this new portrayal with additional grit. He plays Bond more business-like and showcases a stronger will. Gone are the days of Moore's cheesy jokes -- Dalton's Bond is darker and edgier.

Flash forward another decade, and Pierce Brosnan's Bond is even more keen to the sensitivities of himself and those around him. In *Tomorrow Never Dies*, he is genuinely upset over the death of Paris Carver (Terri Hatcher), especially since he is largely responsible. Bond holds Carver's dead body to his own and takes a moment to reflect upon losing her. He doesn't cry -- it's not as heartbreaking as losing his wife -- yet there is more tenderness in this scene than when Teresa died in 1969. Bond does the same with Elektra King's (Sophie Marceau) dead body in *The World is Not Enough*.

The chemistry with the Carver character is rather intriguing. She is married to the film's villain, but she and Bond have a history that the movie references. Whether or not it was a long relationship isn't addressed, but the two expressed strong feelings for each other, and Bond apparently left her. Before they renew their love affair, Carver asks him why he departed.

> Carver: What was it James? [approaching him] Did I get too close? Did I get too close for -- comfort?

> Bond: Yes [They passionately kiss].

Carver: [removing her dress while continuing their passionate kissing] I missed you.[12]

Her character helps convey a softer side of Bond. He isn't heartless. He may be a womanizer who has commitment issues, but he never stops caring.

It should be noted that Bond is helping a woman commit adultery in this scene, which is a reoccurring theme throughout the 007 series. That's obviously not the action of a moral man, but still, through this motif, the series again conveys Bond's perfect masculinity and the villains' deficiencies as men.

Unlike Bond, the villains are evil to the core and often old. They usually aren't attractive -- at least never as sexy as Bond – and usually are out of shape and marked with scars. *You Only Live Twice* reveals Blofeld's face with a horrific scar around his right eye. This concept is repeated with Renard (Robert Carlyle) in *The World is Not Enough* and Le Chiffre (Mads Mikkelsen) in *Casino Royale*.

Sometimes, the villains are gay. In *Diamonds Are Forever* (1971), the Spectre henchmen, Mr. Kidd (Putter Smith) and Mr. Wint (Bruce Glover), hold hands as they walk into the desert while creepy music plays. The film writers want the audience to dislike these villains and find them even more disturbing because they're gay. Their homosexuality is only mentioned in passing and is very unnecessary.

Also, it was another way the writers showcased why the audience should love Bond. He's a man who never leaves any

---

[12] *Tomorrow Never Dies*. Directed by Roger Spottiswoode. 1997. Beverly Hills, CA: MGM/United Artists, DVD.

woman unsatisfied. The heterosexual male loves this fact about Bond, and in turn, *Diamonds Are Forever* is telling its male audience that they shouldn't relate to these villains. The film says their gayness makes them less manly, as they don't even desire women.

This simply wouldn't be accepted nor received the same way by audiences today.

That brings us back to Carver. Bond sleeps with her to get to her husband, Elliot Carver (Johnathan Pryce). 007 repeats this tactic 10 times in the series, as he uses sex to gain the intel he needs to accomplish his mission.

However, if the villains satisfied their girlfriends and wives, the women likely wouldn't stray. The series implies they are missing something in their lives -- both physically and emotionally -- and Bond satisfies that need the less desirable villain leaves unfulfilled.

This is true even with Bond's sexual encounter with Lucia Sciarra (Monica Bellucci) in the film *Spectre* (2015).

> Sciarra: [while passionately kissing Bond] He (her husband) was obsessed. He spent more time with them (the Spectre crime organization) than with me.

> Bond: Then the man was a fool.[13]

---

[13] *Spectre*. Directed by Sam Mendes. 2015. Culver City, CA: Sony Pictures Releasing/Columbia Pictures, DVD.

Curiously, in the case of Paris Carver, it wasn't Bond's idea to take advantage of her. That plan came from M (Judi Dench) and Moneypenny (Samantha Bond).

M: I believe you once had a relationship with Carver's wife, Paris.

Bond: That was a long time ago, M, before she was married. I didn't realize it was public knowledge [delivering a slight glare at Moneypenny].

Moneypenny: Queen and country, James.

M: Your job is to find out whether Carver or someone in his organization sent that ship off course, and why. Use your relationship with Mrs. Carver, if necessary.

Bond: I doubt if she'll remember me.

M: Remind her. Then pump her for information.

Moneypenny: You'll just have to decide how much pumping is needed, James.[14]

This is a rare moment where Bond actually shows a bit of humility. Of course, Paris does remember him. After 007 sleeps with her to gain intel, he has every intention of protecting her. When he fails, he spends a moment with her body following her death.

That's quite different from the early days of the series. The ultimate man is now expressing his feelings and even a little

---

[14] *Tomorrow Never Dies.* 1997.

empathy -- a reflection on how the idea of what was masculine had changed from the 1960's to the 1990's.

This helped make way for the Bond character audiences know and love today. On the surface, Daniel Craig's Bond is as rough and rugged as Connery's portrayal in the 1960's. Under Craig, Bond has returned to his original roots as a cold-hearted killer. There's little to no comedy as well, making Craig the most serious of all the Bonds.

And yet, he's also the most vulnerable, indicating where masculinity stands early in the 21st century.

In Craig's debut film, *Casino Royale*, Bond falls in love with Vesper Lynd (Eva Green). He shows more love and affection for Lynd than he does any other woman in the series -- even his previous wife. This isn't an arranged marriage. Bond and Lynd choose to be together from the start, and 007 isn't afraid to show his affection.

Ironically enough, before Bond and Lynd express their love for each other, 007 almost loses his manhood -- literally. Le Chiffre performs a torture technique called Dutch Scratching, where Bond sits naked in a seatless chair, with his genitalia hanging exposed. Bond refuses to provide Le Chiffre with his bank account password, so Le Chiffre whips 007 where it hurts most.

This scene is in the novel, and with *Casino Royale* being the first story in the series, the testicle torture is supposed to explain why Bond never has kids despite his repetitive sexcapades. But in 2006, the scene helps bring modern masculinity into question. Le Chiffre nearly strips Bond of what fundamentally makes him a man.

For the first time in the series, Bond is truly vulnerable. He wakes up and really doesn't know if he will be adequate in the bedroom again.

It is in this scene where Bond and Lynd express their feelings for each other.

> Lynd: You know, James, [getting emotional] I just want you to know that if all that was left of you was your smile and your little finger, you'd still be more of a man than anyone I've ever met.

> Bond: [leaning closer to her] That's because you know what I can do with my little finger.

> Lynd: [smiles] I have no idea.

> Bond: But you're aching to find out [smirking].

> Lynd: You're not going to let me in there, are you? You've got your armour back on. That's that.

> Bond: I have no armour left. You've stripped it from me. Whatever is left of me -- whatever is left of me -- whatever I am -- I'm yours.[15]

Leave it to Bond to reference sex while he spills his feelings, but this monologue suggests masculinity is about more than sex and violence. Lynd still finds Bond desirable despite his possible inefficiencies. Bond no longer has to be perfect to be an action hero.

---

[15] *Casino Royale.* Directed by Martin Campbell. 2006. Culver City, CA: Sony Pictures Releasing, DVD.

Of course, this relationship doesn't end well. Working as a secret double agent for Quantum, Lynd betrays him and never returns his "I love you." Craig's 007 was already the most humorless, and then Lynd breaks his heart. It's the first unhappy ending in a Bond movie since 1969, and it helps explain why Bond is so cold towards women.

The difference in this heartbreaking ending, though, is Bond showcases his feelings. When Lynd dies in his arms, 007 appears to be on the verge of tears. This happens again when he holds M as she dies at the end of *Skyfall*.

It's thought-provoking to think about why the Bond series made such a drastic change in its hero during the early 2000's. Did the series simply believe it needed to modernize to stay relevant or did something change in masculinity in western society?

More than likely, it was a little of both. Whatever the reason, audiences responded to it.

In the attempt to modernize, rather than drastically changing the character, the series creators and writers portray 007 as flawed. M calls Bond a misogynist for the first time in 1995, and then in 2006, there are countless references to Bond's hyper ego. It's referenced only seldomly in the first 20 films.

Starting in 2006, Bond is no longer perfect, just as masculinity is no longer narrowly defined. It's now socially acceptable for a man to show emotion, cry and care. However, that doesn't mean Craig's Bond openly displays his weaknesses.

In *Skyfall*, he waits for his co-workers to leave before collapsing from doing too many pull-ups while getting back into shape after retirement. In *Spectre,* his love interest, Madeleine Swann (Léa Seydoux) tells 007 she's leaving because she can't deal with his spy life. Despite her departure, he doesn't say a word; he simply watches her walk away and then refocuses on his job.

During *Quantum of Solace* (2008), Bond vehemently denies Lynd meant anything to him in front of Mr. White (Jesper Christensen), but throughout the film, 007 is shown unable to sleep because he continues to think about her.

That's what masculinity has become in the modern era. Male action heroes aren't perfect, but they still don't candidly showcase their shortcomings.

In addition to fragile masculinity, homosexuality is also no longer taboo. That idea comes bubbling to the surface in *Skyfall.*

Raoul Silva (Javier Bardem) has Bond tied to a chair and begins unbuttoning his shirt and caressing his chest. At first, the scene works as another way for the audience to grow more disdain for the villain. In the mind of the straight male, Silva is even more despicable because he's groping Bond.

Well, the scene takes on a far different tone when Silva rubs both his hands on Bond's legs.

> Silva: [while rubbing Bond's thighs] Well, (there's a) first time for everything. Yes?

> Bond: [smirking] What makes you think this is my first time?[16]

---

[16] *Skyfall.* Directed by Sam Mendes. 2012. Culver City, CA: Sony International Pictures, DVD.

When Silva's hands first touch Bond's thighs, 007's face seems taken aback by the gesture. In modern times, this is probably the natural reaction any straight male might have who wouldn't want to offend someone who is homosexual.

But, other than that slight reaction, just like at the Chemin de fer table, 007 keeps his stone face. If he's uncomfortable, he doesn't show it; he's always cool.

Bond's response to the advance is perfect, as the series found a way to make 007 relatable to a gay audience as well. Bond's reply is entertaining the possibility of him being with another man.

Even 57 years after his film debut, all men still want to be Bond, and despite his flaws, women still want him. Now, on top of that, gay men want him too.

This important idea has helped the 007 character remain one of the most popular action heroes early in the 21st century.

2

RISE OF THE ANTI-HERO

The Bond action hero has many successors, but in the 21st century, he might hold the most similarities with a character that's existed even longer than 007.

Although one could classify Bond and Batman, who debuted on film in 1943, into two separate character categories -- action and superhero -- the likeness between the two is astonishing. Both drive a very cool car and use gadgets to defeat their enemies. They were orphans and had plenty of lady friends over the years too.

As far as the acting profession goes, it doesn't get much bigger than playing either Bond or Batman, and several men have donned each character's suit in the last 60 years.

Most importantly, both series followed similar paths to the modern era, rebranding their star as an anti-hero in the mid-2000's.

One stark difference, though, between Bond and Batman is in their stories of origin. While neither film series in the 1960's emphasized how their heroes became orphans, the story of

Batman's parents became a huge focal point for the series beginning in 1989.

For Bond, audiences didn't see his official background story until 2006, and viewers still waited several more years until there were any significant expansions on what he went through as a child. That, though, did become a subject in *Skyfall* and *Spectre*.

During the 1960's, major character development wasn't an important aspect for a film action hero. That's certainly the case for Bond, as he became very popular despite the audience knowing very little about him.

His preferences, though, were always made very clear. 007 enjoys his martini shaken not stirred, loves Bollinger, prefers Dom Perignon when champagne is his drink of choice and uses a Walther PPK at the request of his superior. He casually sleeps with it under his pillow.

Other than that, early audiences are aware of very little from his backstory. While it's somewhat implied, viewers don't truly learn Bond is an orphan until *Goldeneye* in 1995.

Another aspect of the Bond character that audiences initially learn is his misogynistic views of women. Intentionally or not, this is established shortly after his transcendent masculinity is manifested during his debut scene of *Dr. No*.

Not long before his bedroom encounter with Trench, Bond visits the MI6 office and meets Moneypenny (Lois Maxwell) for the first time. Moneypenny and Bond routinely flirt in each film, and in *Dr. No*, after Moneypenny attempts to seduce 007, Bond says he could never be with her because it would be "illegal use of government property."[17] That, though, doesn't stop him from providing her a few pecks on the check before he departs.

Watching this today, it's easy to see the issues with this scene. Comparing women to any type of property, even in a playful manner, is not appropriate. It's probably safe to say the "Me Too" movement wouldn't be a fan of the casual kissing between two co-workers in the workplace either.

These sexist problems arise through the 1960's and into the 1970's. Even as the series finds ways to fade scenes such as these, beginning in the 1980's, the Bond character still remains mostly cold-hearted towards women. Well, on a good day, he's cold-hearted, and at his worst, he's still flat-out misogynistic.

In *Skyfall*, Bond meets Séverine (Berenice Marlohe), ironically enough, at a casino. She is a former sex slave, and the mistress of the film's antagonist, Raoul Silva. Bond uses his instincts to realize she doesn't stay with Silva by choice; in addition to being his mistress, she's essentially his prisoner.

007 may have every intention of saving Séverine, but it's obvious to the audience that he's willing to say or do whatever it takes to convince her to introduce him to Silva. That includes sleeping with her.

Using sex as manipulation isn't exactly the act of a true hero, and especially not when it's knowingly done to a former sex slave. As a result of sleeping with Bond, Silva kills Séverine.

---

[17] *Dr. No.* 1962.

Even his creator, Bond novel author Ian Fleming, didn't fully argue the British spy was a moral compass for good.

"I don't think that he (Bond) is necessarily a good guy or a bad guy." Fleming said to *Playboy* magazine in 1964. "He's got his vices and very few perceptible virtues except patriotism and courage, which are probably not virtues anyway."

Perhaps even more incredibly, Fleming also went on to say, "I didn't intend for him (Bond) to be a particularly likeable person."[18]

If Fleming were alive today, he'd probably be extremely surprised to see that in 2003, the American Film Institution voted Bond the third-best hero in American film history.[19] That's not just action heroes -- but any heroic character in the first 100 years of filmmaking.

With regards to likeability and popularity, it's hard to top 007. Audiences overlooked Séverine's death in 2012, as *Skyfall* was well received among critics and set a franchise record with $1.1 billion at the worldwide box office. Even when taking into account an adjustment to inflation, that's a franchise record. The next edition in the series, *Spectre* didn't do quite as well, but still made $880 million worldwide.[20]

---

[18] Ian Fleming, "Playboy Interview." December 1964 Issue, http://www.the007dossier.com/007dossier/post/2014/12/05/The-Playboy-interview-Ian-Fleming-December-1964.
[19] "AFI's 100 Years … 100 Heroes & Villains," *American Film Institute*, June 4, 2003, https://www.afi.com/100years/handv.aspx.
[20] https://www.boxofficemojo.com/showdowns/chart/?id=craigsbonds.htm.

Bond has become so ingrained in culture, particularly British culture, that Daniel Craig escorted Queen Elizabeth to the Olympics opening ceremony in 2012.

While writing this book, these facts led me to these questions - - what makes Bond so popular? If he's sexist by today's standards, what attracts viewers to the series? Even though they still know so little about him, why do audiences love 007 so much?

The beginning of the solution to these questions may reside in the biggest virtues the Bond character possesses according to Fleming.

Bond displays unwavering loyalty to Queen (amazingly, the same queen for nearly six decades) and country. It's my theory that readers connected with this aspect of the character in the novels, which were released during the Joe McCarthy 1950's. At that time, Bond was western culture's answer to the Communist spies and betrayers that were deemed to be everywhere.

Five years after McCarthy's death when *Dr. No* hit theaters, audiences still related to Bond's ability to be forthright in the middle of the Cold War. No matter the circumstances, Bond's desire to save the day never changes.

Even when 007 finds a former friend or ally on the other side, evil never tempts him. This has been true in every Bond film, and it became a major theme in *Goldeneye*.

In this film, former British agent 006, Alexander "Alec" Trevelyan (Sean Bean), grows tired of the poor recognition of spy life. Instead of saving the world, he devises a plan for revenge by using a satellite to financially ruin London.

> Trevelyan: We're both orphans, James. But while your parents had the luxury of dying in a climbing accident, mine survived the British betrayal and Stalin's execution squads. My father couldn't let himself, or my mother, live with the shame. MI6 figured I was too young to remember. And in one of life's little ironies, the son went to work for the government whose betrayal caused the father to kill himself and his wife.

> Bond: Hence, Janus. The two-faced Roman God come to life.

> Trevelyan: It wasn't God who gave me this face... it was you, setting the timers for three minutes instead of six.

> Bond: Am I supposed to feel sorry for you?

> Trevelyan: No. You were supposed to die for me …. Oh, by the way, I did think about asking you to join my little scheme, but somehow, I knew, 007's loyalty was always to the mission, never to his friend.[21]

It's no coincidence that this is the plotline of the first post-Cold War 007 film. It works again as a reminder that even though not everyone appears to be who they seem, Bond always is what he is perceived to be.

While at times immoral, he's a man that will never be "two-faced." Bond does what he says he's going to do.

---

[21] *Goldeneye.* Directed by Martin Campbell. 1995. Beverly Hills, CA: MGM/UA, United International Pictures, DVD.

In five of the eight 007 films since 1995, betrayal and treason are common themes demonstrated through the villains. The most recent example of this comes in *Skyfall*.

Like Trevelyan, Silva served as an MI6 agent from 1986-1997. M (Judi Dench) called him a brilliant agent, but after he began "operating beyond his brief" and "hacking the Chinese,"[22] as M stated, she traded him to China for the peaceful transfer of six captured British agents.

During his Chinese torture, Silva took a cyanide pill, but it didn't kill him. Instead, it left his face badly disfigured. His master plan in *Skyfall* really only serves as his way of seeking revenge against M.

[talking through a prison cell, as the MI6 has Silva captured]

Silva: [reacting to M's language] Oh, no remorse. [signs] Just as I had imagined.

M: Regret is unprofessional.

Silva: [laughing] Regret is unprofessional? They (the Chinese) kept me for five months in a room with no air. They tortured me, and I protected your secrets. I protected you. But they made me suffer, and suffer ... and suffer. Until I realized, it was you who betrayed me. You betrayed me. So I only had one thing left -- my cyanide capsule in my back left molar. You remember, right? So I broke the tooth, and bit into the capsule .... It burned all of my insides, but I didn't die. [smiling] Life clung to me like a disease. Then, I

---

22 *Skyfall*. 2012.

understood why I had survived. I needed to look in your eyes one last time.

M: Well, I hope it was worth it.[23]

Miranda Frost (Rosamund Pike) in *Die Another Day* and Vesper Lynd in *Casino Royale* are two other examples of British agents committing treason against the MI6 and England. While the series began shortly after the Red Scare, betrayal has never been a bigger theme in 007 than it has been with Pierce Brosnan and Daniel Craig as Bond.

Perhaps 007's friend René Mathis (Giancarlo Giannini) said it best in *Quantum of Solace*.

Mathis: When one's young, it seems very easy to distinguish between right and wrong. But, as one gets older, it becomes more difficult. The villains and the heroes get all mixed up.[24]

This piece of advice Mathis gives Bond stands true for the series overall, as it's gotten harder for the audience to recognize the good from the evil. That's mostly true in the 21st century too, as American and British wars are no longer fought on battle fronts but rather against extremist groups and terrorists.

Despite their disdain for misogyny and other aspects of the character, millennials can still connect to Bond's straightforwardness. An ally's betrayal will remain a relevant theme to audiences for as long as there are deceitful people in existence, especially in positions of power.

---

[23] *Skyfall*. 2012.
[24] *Quantum of Solace*. Directed by Marc Forster. 2008. Culver City, CA: Sony Pictures Releasing, DVD.

Furthermore, even as sexist as 007 can act at times, viewers can still have a certain level of respect for him as a lover and protector. While he rarely has the best interest of the women he sleeps with, Bond sees the bigger picture, and that's always saving the world first. Along the way, he often saves the women too.

In *Thunderball*, Bond repeatedly flirts with Largo's (Adolfo Celi) mistress, Domino. 007 is aware Domino's brother is at the center of Largo's plot to seize two nuclear warheads and use them to extort £100 million from NATO. If they don't pay, Largo will fire one of the warheads at an American or British city, so while Bond definitely finds Domino attractive, his interest in her is professional -- he hopes to use her to stop the bad guys.

After sleeping with her, Bond tells Domino her brother is dead, killed by Largo, and asks for her help in foiling Largo's master plan. Domino realizes Bond is using her and acts disappointed that their sex wasn't real love, but she helps him anyway. Later, Largo discovers Domino is now assisting Bond, but before Largo can kill Domino, 007 makes sure to save her along with NATO from a nuclear explosion.

Another strong example of this comes in *Live and Let Die* (1973). Bond manipulates Solitaire (Jane Seymour), who is the fortune teller and future lover of Kananga (Yaphet Kotto), the film's villain, into sleeping with him. Solitaire uses a deck of tarot cards designed by artist Fergus Hall to predict the future. Bond sneaks into her bed chamber and reminds her the cards say they will be lovers because Solitaire picked the "lover" card when asked about their relationship earlier in the film.

She isn't quite convinced, but the audience can tell Solitaire does believe the cards may be suggesting they will eventually sleep together. Then, Bond has her pick one more card out of the deck in his hands -- again, she selects the "lover" card.

> Bond: [approaching Solitaire from behind] You knew the answer before it was given... strangely enough, somehow, so did I.[25]

Bond and Solitaire then kiss, but as they head to bed, 007 drops the cards from his hand, revealing an entire deck of "lover" cards. Later, he tells Solitaire he "stacked the deck *slightly* in his favor." This works as comedy too, as no wonder he knew the answer "before it was given."[26]

Regardless, the harm is already done. Solitaire was a virgin before their encounter, and with her taking Bond as a lover, she can no longer foresee the future. Basically, she's no longer of any value to Kananga.

It's unclear in the film whether Bond sleeps with her in order to take away her ability to tell Kananga the future or if he simply just jumped at the chance to antagonize his enemy where it would hurt most -- taking away his future lover's virginity.

If one or the other is his main purpose, Solitaire isn't of any use to Bond after their sexual encounter -- 007 got what he wanted. After escaping the crocodile pit towards the end of the film, Bond returns to San Monique and sets off explosives in Kananga's poppy fields, destroying his plan to distribute

[25] *Live and Let Die.* Directed by Guy Hamilton. 1973. Beverly Hills, CA: United Artists, DVD.
[26] *Live and Let Die.* 1973.

heroin for free to bankrupt his competitors and increase the number of addicts, then charge double the price later. Following the explosion, Bond could leave, but instead, he saves Solitaire from her voodoo sacrifice.

Modern-day Bond doesn't possess any superior morals. In *Spectre*, the only lead 007 acquires after killing a man is a ring and the man's wife, Lucia Sciarra. Bond sleeps with Sciarra in an effort to learn more about the secret crime organization her husband worked for during his life.

But the key difference is how the series portrays these acts. In 1965, the filmmakers glorified Bond's ability to use sex as manipulation. Although 007 still does the same today, the series no longer personifies him as the perfect action hero.

While Batman made its anti-hero rebranding obvious with the final monologue of *The Dark Knight* (2008), Bond's transition to anti-hero hasn't been so clear. 007 didn't nobly take the blame for someone else's crimes so an entire town could still look up to a dead politician.

But returning to the overarching theme of chapter one, Bond is flawed in the 21st century. Audiences relate to him not necessarily because of his impeccable masculinity but rather due to his desire to be forthright and loyal -- even if that means he isn't always ethical.

British author Imogen Lloyd Webber agrees with this point, writing in a column for *Fox News* in 2012 that "Bond represents the best of Britain," calling him "fearless, loyal and sexy."[27]

Presenting 007 with flaws also makes him more of a real person. Realism is another major connection between the modern Bond and Batman films, which will be explored further in the chapters to come.

Bond doesn't save every woman he uses for sex, but it's clear that their safety is one of his concerns. Just as he did with Solitaire, he calls his CIA contact, Felix Leiter, to get Sciarra out of danger in *Spectre*.

However cruel and manipulative he can be at times, 007 is a lover and protector at heart. But most importantly, nothing can alter his desire to serve his country -- not friends, women, money, nor fame.

From *The Man with the Golden Gun*:

> Bond: [following a tour of his estate] You live well, Scaramanga.
>
> Francisco Scaramanga: At a million dollars a contract, I can afford to, Mr. Bond. You work for peanuts, a hearty well done from her Majesty the Queen and a pittance of a pension. Apart from that, we are the same. [picking up his drink for a toast] To us, Mr. Bond, we are the best.

---

[27] Imogen Lloyd Webber, "Fearless, loyal and sexy – James Bond represents the best of Britain," *Fox News*, Nov. 9, 2012, https://www.foxnews.com/opinion/fearless-loyal-and-sexy-james-bond-represents-the-best-of-britain.

Bond: There's a useful four-letter word, and you're full of it.[28]

007 has always been loyal to Queen and country, but the series emphasizing that integrity and his protective nature, coupled with his faults, make Bond relatable to viewers of any generation.

---

[28] *The Man with the Golden Gun*. Directed by Guy Hamilton. 1974. Los Angeles, CA: United Artists, DVD.

3

THE 20TH CENTURY DAMSEL IN DISTRESS

While diehard Bond fans will remember Sylvia Trench as the first Bond girl, most would probably give the title to Honey Ryder (Ursula Andress). Ryder first appears in *Dr. No* when Bond visits an island called Crab Key off the coast of Jamaica.

Bond first lays eyes on Ryder as she comes out of the water on the beach wearing only a white bikini. The look on Bond's face when he sees her practically mirrors the faces of all the women who laid eyes on 007 during the beginning of the film. She's got his attention, and he immediately turns on the charm.

In his first attempt to flirt with her, Bond begins singing the same song she is humming. When Ryder is startled as he approaches, he replies with a quick-witted joke. Connery's Bond is known for these.

Ryder: What are you doing here? Looking for shells?

Bond: No, I'm just looking.[29]

---

[29] *Dr. No.* 1962.

More importantly, one of the biggest elements of the 007 movie series -- the Bond girl -- is born.

Through these women, the series also creates one of its most popular reoccurring themes -- the damsel in distress.

Considered to be old-fashioned and even patronizing towards women, the damsel in distress motif isn't unique to the 007 series, but it is used throughout the films. While this first started in *Dr. No*, the latest Bond movie, *Spectre*, also featured this trope.

In total, Bond saves a woman from the clutches of evil during the climactic scene 13 times in the series. In four other films, 007 rescues a woman from the villain at some other point in the story, and on three other occasions, Bond and his female companion are trapped together, and he saves them.

Adding it all up, 20 of the 24 Bond films, including 18 of the last 19, utilize the damsel in distress motif in some form or fashion.

What's most interesting about the usage of this old-fashion literary device is that a majority of the Bond girls are portrayed as strong, independent and adventurous. Ryder is out on her own scoping Crab Key for shells when she meets 007. Not that shell hunting is exactly dangerous, but traveling alone to a deserted place probably wasn't something young women did very often in 1962.

Ryder is hardly unique. In *Goldfinger*, Tilly Masterson (Tania Mallet) seeks revenge for her sister's death, chasing Auric Goldfinger (Gert Frobe) to Geneva. In *Thunderball*, Domino plays a hand in her own rescue, shooting a spear into Largo in the final scene. It's the first major instance where a Bond girl helps save 007.

Then in *You Only Live Twice*, the series introduces the first female agent. Aki (Akiko Wakabayashi) is not only the first Asian Bond girl, but the first female to be portrayed as Bond's equal in their profession.

Female agents become very popular in the series during the 1970's, as *The Man with the Golden Gun*, *The Spy Who Loved Me*, and *Moonraker* all feature a female secret agent in some capacity.

In that sense, the Bond series was quite progressive. But no matter how independent the Bond girls would get, at the end of almost every film, 007 saves them. With this theme, the series conveys the idea that even strong women require a man.

New York psychologist Velleda C. Ceccoli summarized this concept perfectly during a discussion of how the series portrays both genders in a 2013 blog post:

> Bond capitalizes on sexual difference, and the "battle of the sexes." The idea that women want men to be men in the powerful way that Bond is a man – he can protect you, love you, and set you straight when necessary. As well as the idea that men like their women to surrender but put up a fight first, that despite the fact that she appears to be independent, she really needs her man.[30]

---

[30] Velleda C. Ceccoli, "On Men: Shaken and stirred," *Velleda C. Ceccoli Ph.D.*, Oct. 29, 2013, https://www.drceccoli.com/2013/10/on-men-shaken-and-stirred/.

The 1980's kicked off with another typical strong and independent Bond girl in the form of Melina Havelock (Claude Bouquet) in *For Your Eyes Only* (1981). Half-Greek and half-British, Havelock's appearance is stunning, and similar to Tilly Masterson, she spends the movie seeking revenge for the death of her parents. During the final battle, she carries a crossbow, reminiscent of the spear gun which Domino used to kill Largo in *Thunderball* almost two decades earlier.

But in the mid-1980's, the Bond girl character moved away from its typical adventure-seeking woman and showcased more of a "girly girl." The Indiana Jones series, which is known to be inspired from the Bond movies, made the same drastic change. That series featured the ditzy Willie Scott (Kate Capshaw) for comedy relief in the sequel *Temple of Doom* (1984) after the series opened with the adventurous Marion Ravenwood (Karen Allen) in *Raiders of the Lost Ark* (1981).

The first 007 film to feature the ditzy Bond girl was *A View to a Kill* in 1985. The next two movies, *The Living Daylights* and *License to Kill*, also showcased Bond girls who were more likely to paint their nails than fire a crossbow.

There were many issues with the Bond series in the mid- to late-1980's, but this was certainly one of the errors the series made. While the Bond character did become more sensitive in the late 1980's, the women did too, and in many ways, the series' portrayal of women in 1989 was less progressive than it was twenty years earlier.

In 1969, the father of Tracy di Vicenzo forces her into an arranged marriage with Bond, but she desperately resisted before falling in love with 007. Di Vicenzo is one of the most independent women in the series, which is one of the reasons her father explains that he wants her to settle down with a man.

By no means is it without sexist undertones -- because as Ceccoli would say, di Vicenzo does eventually surrender to 007 -- but *On Her Majesty's Secret Service* portrays the love Bond and di Vicenzo share as true. That's demonstrated by the fact Bond refuses his endowment of £1 million from di Vicenzo's father on their wedding day.

Unfortunately in the late 1980's, the Bond girl becomes uninteresting. There is no depth to Stacey Sutton (Tanya Roberts) in *A View to a Kill* (1985). Every other word out of her mouth seems to be "James," -- she yells it with a horrific, screechy voice -- because she can't help herself in any dangerous situation.

The Bond girls in the next two films weren't as annoying but aren't given any more depth, as they are simply just a pretty face or body to admire during the films. Kara Milovy in *The Living Daylights* is flying an airplane for a mere few minutes, and she almost flies it into a giant mountain. I'm no pilot, but generally speaking, if there's an open desert with mountain ranges to the right, you veer more to the left.

The only Bond girl with any individuality in the late 1980's was Pam Bouvier (Carey Lowell) in *License to Kill*, and she shared the Bond girl role in that film with the far less fascinating Lupe Lamora (Talisa Soto).

The early Bond girls were certainly easy on the eyes as well, and they showcased plenty of skin, but the audience connected far better with their adventurous behavior. Displaying women with shallow personalities was a major step backwards in the late 1980's, and it helped to nearly kill the series.

When the series rebooted in 1995, it rightfully returned with the more adventurous Bond girls, Natalya Simonova (Izabella Scorupco) and Xenia Onatopp (Famke Janssen), in *Goldeneye*. In *Tomorrow Never Dies*, the female secret agent came back as well with Colonel Wai Lin (Michelle Yeoh). Just as he did in *The Spy Who Loved Me* with a Russian female secret agent, Bond works with the enemy -- Colonel Wai Lin is a Chinese spy -- as the two put aside their differences to avoid further conflict between their countries.

The female secret agent character returns again in *Die Another Day* with Halle Berry as Jinx, an American agent working with Bond. Just prior to the turn of the century, *The World is Not Enough* featured the extremely attractive Denise Richards as Dr. Christmas Jones, who is an American nuclear physicist.

On one hand, the series' portrayal of Dr. Jones was rather clumsy. Casting Richards (who isn't a particularly good actress) was strange because she looks more like a shallow supermodel than a nuclear scientist. Part of the issue is the Jones character doesn't dress particularly conservatively like a professional scientist likely would.

Regardless, the series was back on track in the late 1990's. Most, if not all, of the Bond girls had depth to their personalities and desired excitement, and other women in the series began sitting in positions of power. The best example of this is Judi Dench becoming M in 1995.

However, the Bond series needed far more changes than just simply giving some female characters an actual purpose to modernize for the 21st century. Because despite the strong, adventurous, independent women, sexism ran rampant early on in the series.

No matter how much personality a Bond girl possessed, during the first several decades of the series, the character was generally inserted into the story solely as an object of desire. This is true for Ryder, who again first appears in only a white bikini, all the way to Jinx, who just like Ryder, comes out of the water wearing only a bathing suit.

Actually, Berry's first appearance, where she walks up the beach to the bar, pays homage to the famous scene. Jinx is wearing an orange bikini but has a knife on her belt loop as Ryder did. Brosnan's Bond doesn't sing, but he breaks the ice because he wants to meet Jinx as much as 007 wanted to talk to Ryder in *Dr. No*.

> Bond: [with Jinx's back turned to him] Magnificent view.[31]

Wearing bikinis on the beach is one thing, but in the 1970's, the Bond girls often sported a skimpy two-piece in the most inopportune times. In *Diamonds are Forever*, *The Man with the Golden Gun*, and *The Spy Who Loved Me*, the women are wearing new bikinis after the villains capture them.

So upon their capture, the villains force these women to don a two-piece bathing suit. For what purpose? It doesn't make

---

[31] *Die Another Day*. Directed by Lee Tamahori. 2002. Beverly Hills, CA: MGM/20th Century Fox, DVD.

sense. How many supervillains keep bikinis in the closet -- at least enough to have the right size for each woman?

Of course, the viewers aren't supposed to put a lot of thinking into these women wearing bikinis. Like Bond, the audience is expected to just enjoy the view.

Certain language from the series is even worse. In *Goldfinger*, before engaging in a conversation with fellow agent Felix Leiter (Cec Linder), Bond shoes away his masseuse by slapping her on the rear end and saying, "Man talk."[32]

A decade and a half later, the series' treatment of women in the workplace hasn't changed. In *Moonraker*, Bond's response to meeting Dr. Goodhead (Lois Chiles) couldn't have been more sexist.

> Bond: My name is Bond, James Bond. I'm looking for Dr. Goodhead.
>
> Dr. Goodhead: You just found her.
>
> Bond: [smirking] A woman?[33]

The most obvious sexism occurs in some of the female character's names such as Dr. Goodhead. Early in the series, it was commonplace for at least one female name in every movie to be a sexual double entendre, and it continued into the 1990's.

---

[32] *Goldfinger*. Directed by Guy Hamilton. 1964. Beverly Hills, CA: United Artists, DVD.

[33] *Moonraker*. Directed by Lewis Gilbert. 1979. Beverly Hills, CA: United Artists, DVD.

List of Double Entendre Female Names

- Sylvia Trench, *Dr. No*
- Honey Ryder, *Dr. No*
- Pussy Galore, *Goldfinger*
- Plenty O'Toole, *Diamonds Are Forever*
- Dr. Goodhead, *Moonraker*
- Octopussy, *Octopussy*
- Xenia Onatopp, *Goldeneye*

While this served mostly as comedy, it's largely offensive to the female audience for obvious reasons. As women gained more power in society late in the 20th century, the double entendre jokes grew less acceptable.

This is one of the biggest sources of comedy in the James Bond spoof series, Austin Powers. The parody trilogy used numerous sexual double entendres for both men and women, which probably helped put an end to these types of jokes in the Bond canon.

But if only a slap on the rear end and a kiss on the cheek for Moneypenny in *Dr. No* were the worst of Bond's actions. In *Goldfinger*, 007 forces himself on Pussy Galore despite her repeatedly rejecting him.

While the film doesn't explicitly portray her as a lesbian like in the novel, there are slight hints that she is homosexual. Pussy's Flying Circus consists of all blonde women, and Galore also tells Bond, "I'm immune to your charms,"[34] perhaps the 1964 way of saying, "I'm not interested because I'm a lesbian."

---

[34] *Goldfinger*. 1964.

But apparently, Bond is like Kramer (Michael Richards) in *Seinfeld* (1989-98) and is capable of making any lesbian straight. 007 gets Galore alone in a barn, and his flirting becomes physical. They essentially begin wrestling, and Bond pins himself on top of Galore. Her hands are on his shoulders, and she tries to push him off, but his strength overpowers her. She finally gives in, and they embrace for a passionate kiss.

It should be noted that following their kiss, Galore puts her arms around Bond, as she's no longer resisting. In 1964, that was probably enough for consent, but watching the scene today, it feels like sexual assault.

Bond forcing himself on Galore in this scene sends a dangerous, confusing message to adolescent boys and girls and wouldn't be a scene acceptable in the 21st century.

The same can be said for a few early scenes in *Thunderball*. Bond forces himself on a nurse, Patricia Fearing (Molly Peters), as she repeatedly refuses. When Bond is tied down to an exercise machine, Fearing even goes as far as to say "it's the safest I've felt all day."[35]

Then, when the exercise machine malfunctions (an evil henchmen sets it on too high of a setting), Bond threatens to go tell the facility's manager about the mistake. Fearing asks him not to do that (otherwise, she will lose her job), which Bond agrees to in exchange for sex. At first, Fearing isn't too wild about the trade, but as all women do, she succumbs to Bond's hyper masculinity.

---

[35] *Thunderball*. Directed by Terence Young. 1964. Beverly Hills, CA: United Artists, DVD.

At best, these scenes are simply outdated. At worst, Bond's actions are grounds for sexual assault or even rape, and obviously, the series was wise to eliminate scenes like these.

Other aggressive physical behavior towards women, such as when Bond slaps his masseuse's rear end in *Goldfinger*, is all too common early in the series too. Connery's Bond routinely pushes or slaps women away from him when he's on the phone for business. On other occasions, 007 slaps women when they don't cooperate and refuse to tell him what he wants.

By no means are the women of the Bond series angels, but a man hitting a woman today is flat-out unacceptable – for any reason. Wisely, the Bond series eliminated its hero resorting to violence against women decades ago.

It took removing Bond's overly aggressive sexual and aggressive behavior, the sexist nicknames and ill-timed bikini scenes to completely modernize the series' portrayal of women. The real shift began in the 1990's.

As previously stated, M becomes female in 1995, and Judi Dench's depiction of the character is arguably the toughest in the series. Her constant critiques of her prized agent help present a more realistic relationship between boss and agent, and it likely encouraged more women viewers.

After calling Bond a misogynist in *Goldeneye*, M attacks hyper masculinity again in *Tomorrow Never Dies*. She has one of the best lines of the film when a British admiral questions her decision to investigate rather than counterattack following an apparent act of war from the Chinese.

Admiral Roebuck: With all due respect, M, sometimes I don't think you have the balls for this job.

M: Perhaps. But the advantage is, I don't have to think with them all the time.[36]

It's probably fair to say most female Bond viewers have wanted to say that to a man at some point in their life. M is a female in a man's world, and the line works as a way to connect with women viewers who work in predominantly male fields.

The 2000's films introduce more powerful females. Up until 1999, Bond girls were often determined and charismatic, but other than sleeping with Bond, they were never unfaithful. Then, the series features three consecutive films with female betrayals; the first being Elektra King in *The World is Not Enough*.

At its core, though, her deception can be credited to Stockholm syndrome. The first true female betrayal comes in *Die Another Day* with Miranda Frost.

Gustav Graves: [with Frost pointing her gun at him] So … Miss Frost is not all she seems.

Bond: Looks can be deceptive.

Gustav Graves: Yes. By the way, did you find out who betrayed you in North Korea?

Bond: Only a matter of time.

---

[36] *Tomorrow Never Dies*. 1997.

> Gustav Graves: You never thought of looking inside your own organization [Frost turns her gun to Bond, revealing she's a double agent]?[37]

On one hand, it's dangerous featuring a two-faced woman because it plays into the conniving stereotype that began all the way back with the Bible story of Adam and Eve, where Eve is the one who helps convince Adam to eat the apple. But if society is truly going to feature gender equality, then women should be portrayed as villainous, unfaithful, heartless and criminal as well.

Frost slept with Bond for the same reason he has taken so many women to bed over the years. She used him.

> Frost: [Bond shoots at her, but his gun is unloaded] It was so good of you to bring your gun to bed with us.

> Bond: Yes, occupational hazard.[38]

Female betrayal peaks in the next film, *Casino Royale*. Eva Green plays Vesper Lynd with such elegance and class, and her betrayal is even more shocking.

Interestingly, Lynd never appears in a bikini. She doesn't have to because she is stunningly beautiful in her evening gown at the poker table.

In the modern Bond, there is the occasional woman in a bikini, but the Bond girls no longer dress in minimal clothing. Instead,

---

[37] *Die Another Day.* 2002.
[38] *Die Another Day.* 2002.

they generally wear luxurious, fashionable attire or the female equivalent of Bond's tuxedo.

In fact, Bond is shown without clothes more often in the newer films than the women. Just like Ryder and Jinx before him, Bond walks out of the water onto the beach wearing a skimpy bathing suit in *Casino Royale*.

This is another way the series has modernized itself. Inserting Craig's nude body works as a shallow way to convey Bond's manhood, but it's also a cheap way for the series to gain female viewers. It's no different than the way the series earned its male audience in the 1960's.

His body alone can make 007 an object of desire, and the audience is attracted to the Bond girls based on their charisma and charm. In 1962, those roles were reversed.

The series has taken even more steps to transform its portrayal of women this decade. In *Spectre*, Bond finally sleeps with a woman over 40 years old (Lucia Sciarra). While she appears much younger, Monica Bellucci, who plays Sciarra, was 50 years old at the time of the film's release.

"I can't say I'm a Bond girl because I'm too mature to be a Bond girl," Bellucci said in an interview with *The Guardian* in 2015. "I say Bond lady; Bond woman."[39]

The series underutilized Bellucci's talent, and because she was a mere one-night stand, reviewers heavily criticized the scene.

---

[39] Monica Bellucci. "30 Minutes with Monica Bellucci," Interview by Nigel M. Smith, *The Guardian*, Sept. 17, 2015, https://www.theguardian.com/film/2015/sep/17/monica-bellucci-james-bond-spectre-bond-woman.

But for female fans, especially older ones, the brief inclusion of Bellucci was extremely important.

"Men think that women, when they're not able to procreate anymore, become old," Bellucci told *The Guardian*. "That is not true - they are still amazing. That's why I think that Sam Mendes (director of *Spectre*), in choosing me, an adult woman, created a big revolution."[40]

Another revolution may be coming to the Bond films. In December 2018, the series announced Léa Seydoux will be back to reprise her role as the latest Bond girl, Dr. Madeleine Swann.[41]

The only other actress to make a return as the same Bond girl is Eunice Gayson as Sylvia Trench, and she only appeared in one scene during *From Russia with Love* (1963). The original plan was to make Trench the steady girlfriend of Connery's Bond, but her character was scratched from the series following the second film.

In a series known for its beautiful Bond girls -- or to be politically correct, Bond women -- featuring a reoccurring female lead is a major deal. But it's necessary for the series to stay current as 007 approaches his seventh decade on screen.

Even with its continued use of the damsel in distress motif, more women are going to see Bond films. Forty-six percent of

---

[40] Monica Bellucci, "30 Minutes with Monica Bellucci."

[41] Baz Bamigboye, "Lea Seydoux will star in ANOTHER James Bond after director and 007 actor Daniel Craig asked her to come back for next adventure Bond 25," *Daily Mail*, December 6, 2018, https://www.dailymail.co.uk/tvshowbiz/article-6469437/Lea-Seydoux-star-James-Bond-director-Daniel-Craig-asked-come-back.html.

the audience that saw *Spectre* on its opening weekend were women, which was a six percent increase from *Skyfall*.[42]

All of the ways in which the series has changed its portrayals of females have helped Bond grow more popular among women, and the return of Seydoux only indicates the producers are ready to do more to cater to the female audience.

---

[42] Anthony D'Alessandro, "'Spectre' $70.4M Opening: Still 2nd Highest 007 Debut Behind 'Skyfall', But Not That Far From 'Quantum of Solace,'" *Deadline*, November 9, 2015, https://deadline.com/2015/11/spectre-the-peanuts-movie-james-bond-box-office-1201610575/.

4

"BE CAREFUL OF HER NAIL POLISH"

The third woman, Miss Taro (Zena Marshall), Bond sleeps with in his debut film, *Dr. No*, is not nearly as notable as Sylvia Trench or Honey Ryder, but like her other two counterparts, Miss Taro helps set a standard for the entire series.

In *Dr. No*, Bond catches Miss Taro spying on his conversation with her boss through a peephole in the wall. Aware that she isn't all that she seems, Bond sees a lead and asks her to be his tour guide of the island. She initially says maybe, but then she calls his hotel and invites Bond to her house in the countryside.

> Miss Taro: What should I say to an invitation from a strange gentleman?
>
> Bond: You should say yes.
>
> Miss Taro: [shaking her head] I should say maybe.[43]

Miss Taro has no intention of showing Bond a good time, as the three assassins working for Dr. No are planning to intercept 007

---

[43] *Dr. No*. 1962.

on his route to her house and kill him. The only problem is Bond smells the trap and kills the assassins first.

So when Bond arrives at her house, Miss Taro is completely off guard, wearing only a towel. This makes Bond more suspicious, so he invites himself inside and tries to seduce her. But a phone call interrupts them -- Miss Taro answers, and while the audience never learns who's on the other end, the viewers can deduce it's someone else she's taking orders from, and her new orders are to keep 007 around until a new assassin can arrive.

Now Miss Taro is very interested in some bedroom fun. They have sex twice while waiting for the assassin, and in the meantime, Bond has set his own little trap. He asks Miss Taro to go to a restaurant, and she agrees, hoping the assassin will be waiting in the house when they return. Except, Bond didn't call a cab, but rather, a police car. Miss Taro gets into the car thinking she's on her way to dinner, and instead, she's off to the police station.

As if taking advantage of her for sex wasn't enough, Bond provides one more dig before she heads to prison.

"Be careful of her nail polish,"[44] he tells the policeman.

With Miss Taro heading to the police station, Bond waits around for the assassin to arrive, tricks him into thinking he's sleeping and then kills him on the spot. For 1962, it's a rather complex scheme, but Miss Taro works as the series' first femme

---

[44] *Dr. No*. 1962.

fatale, and her character sets a tone for how sex is used throughout the rest of the films.

This is one of 20 examples where Bond either sleeps with the enemy or the antagonist's girlfriend throughout the series. The films repeat this for several reasons. Again, it conveys Bond's superior masculinity over the antagonists. Furthermore, it showcases Bond's spy abilities and enables him to engage in fun, meaningless sex.

In early Bond films, sex either has nothing to do with the plot or is only used as a plot device. In *Dr. No*, sex with Trench and Ryder is pointless -- the story would stay the same without it, as it really only works to display Bond's prowess with the ladies. Meanwhile, Bond's sexual encounter with Miss Taro is only a plot device, as it helps 007 get closer to his objective of catching the villain.

The other main purpose of the sex is for the audience. The heterosexual male viewer wants the women while the heterosexual female audience desires Bond.

Interestingly, viewers seem to accept the idea of meaningless sex more readily in 1962 than 2012. Even with premarital sex growing more popular in the latter part of the 20th century, the 007 series has actually featured less promiscuity in recent years.

Every 1960's film in the series has an example of Bond exploiting a woman for his job. The real reason he forces himself on Galore in *Goldfinger* is to convince her to help him foil Goldfinger's master plan. After one sexual encounter in a barn, she does exactly that.

Bond sleeps with Domino in *Thunderball* for the same reason. He gains valuable intel because Domino is Largo's mistress.

In *Goldfinger*, Bond also sleeps with Jill Masterson (Shirley Eaton). 007 meets her when he sneaks into Goldfinger's hotel suite in Miami and discovers Goldfinger has been cheating at gin. Their sex comes after Bond has already performed his duty, so this bedroom conquest is for pleasure. However, the villain's top henchman, Oddjob (Harold Sakata) kills Masterson, and their encounter becomes a plot device.

Masterson was only the first "sacrificial lamb" -- a Bond girl, who, after dating or working for a villain, meets her death because she sleeps with and/or helps 007. This occurs five times throughout the series.

The next example of this happens in *The Man with the Golden Gun*. In the middle of the film, Bond is about to sleep with long-time co-worker and fellow spy, Mary Goodnight (Britt Ekland), but instead, he rushes her into the closet because Andrea Anders (Maud Adams), who is the mistress of Francisco Scaramanga (Christopher Lee), the villain of the film, knocks on Bond's door asking for help. Rather than Goodnight, Bond sleeps with Anders as a way of offering his assistance in exchange for information.

After Anders leaves, he turns his charm back towards Goodnight, who's been in the closet for hours. This is notable for two reasons. Firstly, it's one of the better examples of how the series conveys the acceptance of multiple sexual partners.

Another case of this is when Bond casually engages in a threesome with two Gypsy women during *From Russia with*

Love. As repayment for Bond saving his life, Vavra (Francis De Wolff), who is head of the Gypsy tribe, offers two women for 007 to take to his chamber. Bond's Turkish contact, Kerim Bey (Pedro Armendáirz), brings both women.

> Bey: Vavra said for you to decide, so decide. They are both yours [leaves laughing].

> Bond: This might take some time.[45]

Ultimately, Bond doesn't decide, as he has both women that night, and then the next morning, each woman serves him. This scene not only encourages multiple sex partners, but it also conveys the notion that women are property, offered to men in the same way someone might offer a friend a drink to express gratitude. Property that, following sex, should wait on their man.

Secondly, 007's courtship of Anders in *The Man with the Golden Gun* showcases yet another Bond girl's betrayal. Scaramanga kills her when he discovers her adultery, making her another sacrificial lamb.

More than 20 years later, the Paris character in *Tomorrow Never Dies* works in the same fashion. The sex is largely meaningless, but it leads to the woman's death. This gives the audience another reason to root for Bond to kill the villain.

In *Casino Royale*, Bond takes Solange (Caterina Murino), who is married to one of Le Chiffre's evil stooges, Alex Dimitrios (Simon Abkarian), back to his hotel room for what looks like

---

[45] *From Russia With Love*. Directed by Terence Young. 1963. Beverly Hills, CA: United Artists, DVD.

another sexual encounter. But Solange tells Bond what he needs to know before the sex occurs.

> Solange: [laying on top of Bond] Apparently, he's (Dimitrios) on the last flight to Miami. So, you have all night to question me.

> Bond: [kissing her] In that case, we're gonna need - some more champagne [disengaging their kissing].

> [after dialing phone for room service]

> Bond: Good evening. Could I get a bottle of chilled Bollinger and the beluga caviar? [person on phone asks "For two?"] No, for one.[46]

In this instance, the filmmakers portray Bond a little less heartless, as he doesn't sleep with Solange to gain his intel. But the result is the same -- because he used her, Solange ends up murdered.

It's an intriguing debate whether this seemingly more modern approach is any better. Are Bond's tactics more justified because he didn't use Solange for his own sexual pleasure? Before answering, one should probably also consider the hypothetical where Solange doesn't provide Bond the intel he needs prior to their sex. There's a very good chance 007 would have stayed with Solange as long as necessary, having sex with her if he needed in order to find out what was required.

Perhaps what that calls attention to is how differently Bond views sex versus how the series does in 2006. Bond's

---

[46] *Casino Royale.* 2006.

perspective on meaningless sex has largely stayed the same over five decades -- he loves women, but generally, he doesn't let them distract him from completing his missions.

But in the 1960's, the audience seems to more readily connect to Bond's sexual prowess as a fantasy. Contrary to popular belief, a study conducted in the United States suggests pre-martial sex has been popular for decades, but generally, Americans have been more open about discussing it in recent years.[47]

The openness around pre-martial sex may have, ironically, indirectly helped decline the need for Bond's multiple sex partners in each film. Because society has become more open about sex, maybe it's somewhat lost its fantasy appeal.

Around the same time when the Bond character grew more sensitive, which was in the late 1980's, the series also had to deal with the emergence of AIDS. The spread of the disease at that time impacted the series, leading to fewer engagements of casual sex.

Well aware of the concern for AIDS victims in 1987, Screen Actors Guild spokesman Mark Locher, who closely worked on *The Living Daylights*, told *The Chicago Tribune*:

"There was a conscious effort to portray the new Bond as not someone who sleeps with every woman he meets, and as one

---

[47] Lawrence B. Finer, "Trends in Premarital Sex in the United States, 1954-2003," *Public Health Reports*, April 18, 2019, https://www.ncbi.nlm.nih.gov/pmc/articles/PMC1802108/.

who values monogamy. There was the feeling the public wouldn't stand for it otherwise."[48]

This is interesting, because again, pre-martial sex is more generally accepted in the younger generations. Yet, the series producers have strayed from Bond sleeping with multiple women in each film.

Unlike in the 1960's, there were feelings attached to Bond's lovemaking during the late 1980's. In *License to Kill*, he still sleeps with two women. Both apparently have strong feelings for him, and Bond has to choose to solely be with one at the end of the film, and his decision comes with a broken heart for the one he doesn't choose.

That's quite different from Bond's threesome days in *From Russia with Love*.

In *Goldeneye*, there's more of a romantic tone when Bond is with Natalya Simonova than in any of the previous films. In the middle of the movie, Alec Trevelyan threatens to kill Simonova, but Bond quickly says that she means nothing to him. When the story returns to this idea, it is apparent that this was a lie.

> Simonova: [laying in bed on top of Bond] On the train, when you told him to kill me, and that I meant nothing to you, did you mean it?

---

[48] Mark Locher, "AIDS Awareness writes casual sex out of move, television scripts," *The Chicago Tribune*, June 25, 1987, https://www.chicagotribune.com/news/ct-xpm-1987-06-25-8702160902-story.html.

Bond: Yes. Basic rule -- always call their bluff. [Simonova begins hitting him with a pillow in a joking manner].[49]

Anybody who's seen the film knows Bond is just being coy with that answer. He does appear to deeply care for Simonova during their love scenes, helping to express the idea that Bond isn't as much of a womanizer as he was early in the series.

Surely, he still gets around though. At the beginning of both *The Living Daylights* and *Tomorrow Never Dies*, Bond engages in sex with a woman that the series doesn't even bother to introduce with a name.

From *The Living Daylights*:

Woman on boat in bikini: [while talking on the phone] It's all so boring here, Margo -- there's nothing but playboys and tennis pros. [signs] If only I could find a real man.

[Bond lands on her boat in a smoldering parachute]

Bond: I need to use your phone. [takes phone from her and says into it] She'll call you back.

Woman [listed as Linda in the credits]: Who are you?

Bond: Bond, James Bond. [into phone] Exercise Control, 007 here. I'll report in an hour.

Linda: [offering champagne] Won't you join me?

Bond: [smiling into phone] Better make that two (hours).[50]

---

[49] *Goldeneye.* 1995.
[50] *The Living Daylights.* Directed by John Glen. 1987. Beverly Hills, CA: MGM/United Artists, United International Pictures, DVD.

The film then cuts to the opening credits and never shows the woman again. Of course, the film doesn't explicitly state Bond and the woman have sex, but based on the opening of this dialogue, her typical Bond girl attire along with 007's response and smile, it's implied.

However, there was nothing hidden about Bond's sexual encounter with Oxford Professor Inga Bergstrom (Cecilie Thomsen) during *Tomorrow Never Dies*. Her name is also not revealed (only mentioned in the credits), and she didn't get any clothes either. The first time the audience sees Bergstrom, she is teaching Bond some Danish in bed.

> Bergstrom: [speaking in Danish during lovemaking] I am pleased with your progress, Mr. Bond.
>
> Bond: [answering slowly in Danish while continuing to kiss] I've always enjoyed studying a new tongue, Professor.
>
> Bergstrom: [in Danish while kissing] One might say you have a natural ability.
>
> Bond: [in Danish while kissing] But practice makes perfect.[51]

So while 007's sex with the main Bond girls is more meaningful by the late 1980's, the films still display him engaging in meaningless sex elsewhere. Just like with Trench in the first two films, these two examples of sexual encounters serve no purpose to the plot.

---

[51] *Tomorrow Never Dies*. 1997.

The other major issue with sexuality in the Bond series is the often wide age gap between 007 and his sexual partners. The average age of each Bond girl through the first 20 films is about 28.5. This becomes a problem when Roger Moore plays 007 until he's 57 years old.

At the end of his run, Moore is nearly twice their age and a lot more in some cases. In *For Your Eyes Only*, Carole Bouquet, who plays Melina Havelock, is 23 and Moore is 53. In *A View to a Kill*, Tanya Roberts plays Stacey Sutton at 29, and Moore is 57.[52]

He's old enough to be their father. The women don't have a wrinkle in sight while there were rumors Moore had to wear a toupee.[53] This contributes to the western stereotype that men maintain their sex appeal longer than women.

But similar to the portrayals of masculinity and femininity, the series alters its representation of sexuality in the 21st century. For one, the number of sexual partners for Bond decreases significantly, and subsequently, the amount of meaningless sexual encounters drops too.

In his four movies, Craig's Bond sleeps with an average of 1.5 women per film. Over the first 20 films, the five actors who played Bond took an average of 2.6 women to bed.[54]

Only one film of the first 20 has 007 sleeping with just one woman. Of Craig's four cinematic adventures as Bond, he's had just one sexual partner twice.

---

[52] https://www.mi6community.com/discussion/927/list-of-age-differences-between-bond-and-lead-female.

[53] https://www.imdb.com/title/tt0090264/trivia.

[54] https://en.wikipedia.org/wiki/Bond_girl#List_of_Bond_girls.

Remember, Moore's Bond attempted to sleep with two women on the same night.

Because he passes on the chance to sleep with Solange, Bond only has sex with Lynd in *Casino Royale*, and he falls in love with her. 007 doesn't recover from her betrayal quickly, as he then only takes one lady to his bedchamber again in the next film *Quantum of Solace*.

Fascinatingly, *Quantum of Solace* is the only Bond film to have its female lead not sleep with 007. Ukrainian actress Olga Kurylenko plays the Bond girl of the film, Camille Montes, but she doesn't become a love interest for Bond, suggesting that he is still grieving from his lost love.

Quantum of Solace is widely considered to be Craig's weakest Bond film, but it's still refreshing to see an action movie without the predictable entangled love story.

Bond sleeps with Strawberry Fields (Gemma Arterton) in the film to keep his "sex streak" intact, but there's also a purpose to it. Fields is a British operative ordered to bring Bond back to London. He convinces her to let him stay on his assignment, though, with his traditional ways of persuasion.

007 has a pair of sexual encounters in each of the next two films, and just one of the four encounters could be considered truly meaningless. Towards the beginning of *Skyfall*, Bond sleeps with an unnamed female character. Bond is presumed dead and retired on a tropical island. This meaningless sex serves as a way to show how worthless 007 feels about his life in retirement. In that sense, for the film, the meaningless sex isn't

all that inconsequential, as it plays a small purpose for character development.

In two of his other three encounters, Bond exploits the women for information. Obviously, this does not free the series of all sexist criticism -- in these two encounters, he sleeps with a former sex slave, Sévérine in *Skyfall*, and Sciarra's widow Lucia Sciarra, in *Spectre*. Both sexual occurrences are far from true love, and in the case of Sévérine, she succumbs to her death because she gets caught as 007's lover and partner.

Sévérine's death is no different from Masterson in *Goldfinger*, Anders in *The Man with the Golden Gun*, or Paris in *Tomorrow Never Dies*. But from a sexuality perspective, the lovemaking for Craig's Bond always serves a purpose.

Admittedly, Bellucci's Sciarra is underutilized, but her appearance still makes history as the first 50-year-old Bond woman. The average age of the women (based on the actress' ages upon movie release) Craig's 007 sleeps with is 31.[55] It's a small increase from 28.5, but a lot of those women early in the series looked younger than they really were. In general, the series has done a better job of eliminating an awkward age gap and conveying the idea that women older than 35 can still be sexy.

By the end of *Spectre*, Bond is in love again. This time, Dr. Madeleine Swann has his heart.

Like with Lynd, this isn't sex disguised as love. Swann acts a little uninterested as Lynd did upon her first meeting Bond in

---

[55] https://en.wikipedia.org/wiki/Bond_girl#List_of_Bond_girls.

Casino Royale. But just like Lynd, Swann yields to his temptation, and the feeling is mutual.

It's no Dutch Scratching, but Ernst Blofeld (Christoph Waltz), the villain of *Spectre*, tortures Bond with a complex brain operation, which is intended to ruin his memory. If it had worked, it would have been tragic for Swann because she is truly beginning to care for 007.

> Swann: [caressing Bond in a torture chair] I love you...
>
> Blofeld: Do those blue eyes still recognize you?
>
> Bond: [whispering to Swann] I'd recognize you anywhere.[56]

As he usually does, Bond rescues Swann in the film's climactic scene. While it's the 20th example of the "damsel in distress" in the series, this one feels different.

The Craig Bond has experienced so much loss through four films, the audience can't help but feel pleased he ends this adventure with a female for which he genuinely cares. In many ways, this expresses the idea that no matter how badly love can hurt, one can still find and experience love again.

That simply isn't a message the Bond series would have conveyed early in its history. But with the changes in sexual culture through the years, the 007 films adapted well, making Bond's desire for love, and not just sex, a major theme to the series in the 21st century.

---

[56] *Spectre*. 2015.

5

007'S "POSITIVELY SHOCKING" HUMOR

Sex and violence are the two biggest cornerstones of the Bond film series, but humor is a major aspect too. Whether a sexual pun or just a good, old-fashion clean play on words, 007 fans have come to expect several wise cracks from their favorite agent in every single one of his adventures.

In a lot of cases, the jokes are predictable. Yet, they are still enjoyable.

Before the opening credits of *Goldfinger*, Bond destroys a drug laboratory in Latin America and then meets a female dancer in the bathroom. They begin kissing, but the dancer has double crossed him, and a local thug tries a surprise attack.

Bond notices in time to avoid the thug's first punch and engages in a bathroom brawl with the man. This scene actually has nothing to do with the film's plot, but it serves as another action sequence for the audience to enjoy.

Towards the end of the brawl, Bond throws the thug into a tub filled with water. At the beginning of the scene, 007 placed his Walther PPK right above the tub so he could more easily embrace the dancer. Thinking quickly, before the thug can grab the gun, Bond throws a powered electric fan into the tub, electrocuting him.

Bond only mutters one thing as he grabs his Walther PPK and leaves, looking at the dancer one more time.

"Shocking. Positively, shocking."[57]

These obvious puns were common early in the series and helped further the idea that the films were more fun than anything else. But as the series aged and began to take a more realistic approach, humor took a backseat to violence and sex.

Similar to sexuality in the series, there was a drastic change in the humor starting with *Casino Royale* although throughout the series, there were gradual adjustments. Whether it was through the writing or acting, there's a distinct difference between the humor Connery brought to the series versus Moore's comedy.

With Connery, Bond would certainly make wise cracks, but generally, his jokes were more witty and clever. In *From Russia with Love*, Bond's Turkish contact, Kerim Bey, fatally shoots a Soviet assassin, who was trying to climb through a billboard. The billboard is an early example of product placement, as it's actually an advertisement for another Harry Saltzman and Albert R. Broccoli production. The photo on the billboard depicts star Anita Ekberg.

It just so happens that the trap door of the billboard where the assassin is climbing through when he gets shot is in the middle

---

[57] *Goldfinger*. 1964.

of Ekberg's lips. Once the bullet hits him, and he falls to his death, Bond has a great one-liner.

"She should have kept her mouth shut."[58]

While there's a hint of sexual undertones to the joke, it's clever regardless if a viewer takes it to be sexual or not. Quick, witty lines such as these help showcase the charm and debonairness of Bond, who also expresses amusement in the face of danger.

Thunderball has a couple more examples of these. Bond nearly gets into hot water when he mistakenly calls Dominique by her nickname, but again thinking quickly on his feet, 007 has a great response.

Bond: My dear, uncooperative Domino.

Domino: How do you know that? How do you know my friends call me Domino?

Bond: It's on the bracelet on your ankle.

Domino: So … what sharp little eyes you've got [walks away].

Bond: (to himself) Wait 'til you get to my teeth.[59]

This one is more overtly sexual, but it's the same type of quick, clever joke that was common with Connery as Bond. One could describe these more like quips than puns.

---

[58] *From Russia with Love.* 1963.

[59] *Thunderball.* 1964.

The same can be said when Bond tells Largo that his gun isn't quite right.

> Bond: That gun, it looks more fitting for a woman.

> Largo: You know much about guns, Mr. Bond?

> Bond: No, but I know a little about women.[60]

Even when he's trapped in *You Only Live Twice*, Connery's Bond always has one of these quips up his sleeve.

> Helga Brandt (the femme fatale of the film): [with Bond tied to a chair with his hands behind his back] I've got you now.

> Bond: Well, enjoy yourself.[61]

These lines, which, by the way, aren't derogatory towards women, helped make Connery the Bond with the most confidence. But that doesn't mean the 1960's Bond films weren't completely free of demeaning, overly-apparent sexual puns too.

The scene in *Goldfinger* when Pussy Galore reveals her name, and Bond simply murmurs, "I must be dreaming"[62] is one of the most famous scenes in the series' history. While Bond's response is funny, the real joke is her name, and that pun couldn't be any more obviously sexual.

---

[60] *Thunderball*. 1964.
[61] *You Only Live Twice*. Directed by Lewis Gilbert. 1967. Beverly Hills, CA: United Artists, DVD.
[62] *Goldfinger*. 1964.

The same can be said for another exchange between Bond and the femme fatale in *You Only Live Twice*.

Brandt: Mr. Osato (her boss) believes in a healthy chest.

Bond: [while looking at her breasts] Really?[63]

Diamonds are Forever, which was Connery's last time playing Bond in the canon series, featured the most ridiculous breast double entendre of the 007 films.

O'Toole: [while bending over so her cleavage is showing] Hi, I'm Plenty.

Bond: But of course you are.

O'Toole: Plenty O'Toole.

Bond: Named after your father perhaps?[64]

This monologue actually combines the two distinct types of humor early in the Bond series. Viewers who don't find O'Toole's lines funny are probably going to roll their eyes because it's so clearly a sexual pun. But Bond's response is another example of Connery's quick, clever wit. The opening joke couldn't be any more demeaning towards women, but Bond himself finds a way to complete the joke in a non-derogatory way.

While the sexual puns have always existed in the Bond series, obvious jokes such as these became more common in the 1970's and especially increased when Moore became Bond in 1973.

---

[63] *You Only Live Twice*. 1967.

[64] *Diamond Are Forever*. Directed by Guy Hamilton. 1971. Beverly Hills, CA: United Artists, DVD.

Other than additional puns, though, Moore's humor is generally cheesier. Rather than a clever response like the ones Connery delivered, Moore's Bond hits the joke right on the head.

The series introduces the more cheesy humor -- similar to Connery's "positively shocking" line -- in Moore's very first scene of *Live and Let Die*.

> [Bond unzips the back of Miss Caruso's dress with the magnet in his watch].
>
> Miss Caruso: Such a delicate touch.
>
> Bond: Sheer magnetism, darling.[65]

At the end of the film, 007 shoves a gas pellet in the mouth of Kananga, the villain of the film, causing him to inflate with air and explode. He delivers another corny quip.

> Solitaire: Where's Kananga?
>
> Bond: Well, he always did have an inflated opinion of himself.[66]

But this slight change has more to do with the direction of humor in the 1970's as opposed to the different ways the two actors portrayed Bond. There's a much wider emphasis on overt puns during 007's second decade of film.

At the end of *Moonraker*, a video of Bond and Dr. Goodhead together in bed appears on screen for M and the rest of the

---

[65] *Live and Let Die*. 1973.
[66] *Live and Let Die*. 1973.

British secret service. Q is there as well, but he doesn't see the video feed. Instead, he is looking at Bond's spaceship on the radar screen. Q then delivers one of the series' most classic sex puns.

"I think he's attempting re-entry, sir."[67]

The beginning of this film starts with a similar sex pun. Moneypenny tells M that Bond will be returning soon, as he's on the last *leg* of his trip, and then the film cuts to a scene where Bond is fondling a woman's leg.

But Bond in the 1970's is cheesy even when he isn't uttering a sex pun. There's another scene in *Moonraker* where 007 has tossed a henchman through the top of a clock and down several stories, where he lands on a piano, smashing it in pieces.

Bond then says, "Play it again, Sam."[68]

During this decade, the series has only one sex pun that isn't cheesy, but it's a very memorable one, as it's the last line of *The Spy Who Loved Me*. Bond and Anya Amasova escape death in a water pod, which drifts on the ocean to the front of a British battleship. When the two agents' superiors get a look inside the pod, Bond and Amasova are naked together under a blanket.

> Sir Frederick Gray, Minister of Defense: Bond, what do you think you're doing?
>
> Bond: Keeping the British end up, sir [He closes the blinds].[69]

---

67 *Moonraker*. 1979.
68 *Moonraker*. 1979.
69 *The Spy Who Loved Me*. 1977.

Moving into the 1980's, the humor of the series grew even sillier with the use of parodies. Early in *For Your Eyes Only*, Bond cannot use his own Aston Martin to escape because it explodes, so he and Melina Havelock use her ugly, yellow Beetle-looking French economy car. This works as a parody of the Bond series itself, as the audience can find some humor in the fact he has to resort to using a common automobile to escape rather than his gadget-filled car.

In *Octopussy* (1983), 007 leaves a sticky situation swinging on a tree limb, and while swinging, the film plays Tarzan's famous yell from one of his early Hollywood movies. Then in *A View to a Kill*, Bond snowboards his way down the wintry slopes of Siberia to the Beach Boys' famous song, "California Girls".

While both are funny to a viewer of a certain age, these second two examples are over the top, and heading into the 1990's, the humor in the Bond series needed a reset. With the arrival of Pierce Brosnan, that's exactly what happened.

The series eliminated these parodies and returned to focusing on the cheesy puns. With Brosnan, there were also more jokes that didn't feature a double sexual meaning.

In *Tomorrow Never Dies*, Bond fights a henchman in a newspaper facility. To kill him, 007 throws him into the printing machine, and the henchman's blood spills all over the next day's paper.

Bond then says, "They'll print anything these days."[70]

---

[70] *Tomorrow Never Dies*. 1997.

When the series did use sexual puns during the 1990's, the language wasn't quite as obvious as "Pussy Galore" or a re-entry joke. In *Die Another Day*, the first conversation between Bond and Jinx is almost entirely sexual, but it's not to the point where parents of 13-year-old kids have explaining to do after the scene. With the series taking a more subtle approach to their innuendos, there's a chance young teenagers wouldn't even get the jokes.

[Jinx swims up to shore on the beach and then grabs a towel to dry off. Bond is behind her at the bar].

Bond: Magnificent view [drinks mojito].

Jinx: It is, isn't it? Too bad it's lost on everybody else.

Bond: Mojito? [takes a sip of his own drink] You should try it [hands it to her].

Jinx: [extends her hand] Giacinta Johnson. My friends call me Jinx.

Bond: My friends call me James Bond. Jinx you say?

Jinx: Born on Friday the 13th.

Bond: You believe in bad luck?

Jinx: Let's just say my relationships don't seem to last.

Bond: Hmm, I know the feeling [looks over at a man with a woman in his lap and gun in his hand]. Predators usually appear at sunset.

Jinx: [smirking] And why is that?

Bond: It's when their prey comes out to drink. [Jinx tries the mojito] Too strong for you?

Jinx: I can learn to like it. If I had the time.

Bond: How much time have you got?

Jinx: Until dawn. What about you?

Bond: Oh, I'm just here for the birds. [picks up a pair of binoculars] Ornithologist.

Jinx: Ah, ornithologist, huh. [looks down at his crotch] Wow. Now, there's a mouthful.[71]

When Bond meets Dr. Christmas Jones, she is not nearly as receptive to humor. The man who introduces Jones to Bond, who is undercover as a Russian nuclear scientist, tells 007 Jones is not interested in men. Then when Jones says her first name is Christmas, she warns Bond to not make any jokes about it.

Bond is receptive to her wishes, saying he doesn't know any doctor jokes.

She discovers his real identity shortly thereafter and helps him foil Elektra King's plan to destroy Istanbul and the Russian oil pipeline in Turkey. In classic damsel in distress fashion, Bond rescues Jones on a submarine and prevents a nuclear explosion.

At the conclusion of the film, Bond and Dr. Jones are having a romantic night together when finally, 007 lets out a couple Christmas puns.

---

[71] *Die Another Day.* 2002.

Bond: (I've) Always wanted to have Christmas in Turkey.

Jones: Is that a Christmas joke?

Bond: From me? No, never.

Jones: So isn't it time to unwrap your present?

Bond: Oh, I think so [They kiss].[72]

In the very next scene, the two are in bed together, and Bond delivers perhaps the dirtiest pun of the series.

Bond: I was wrong about you.

Jones: Yeah, how so?

Bond: I thought Christmas only comes once a year.[73]

This exchange can be viewed with two different lenses. The more obvious one -- the argument most women would probably make -- is at that point, the series hadn't changed one bit. A woman not at all interested in men still falls head over heels for Bond's masculinity, and he rewards her with several off-colored sexual puns during their first lovemaking session.

But digging a bit deeper and having context with where the series was 30 years prior, this takes on a different tone. In the 1960's, Bond probably would have made this joke a lot earlier in his relationship with Jones. But in 1999, the fact Bond doesn't uncork a sexual Christmas pun until she's already made one

---

72 *The World is Not Enough.* 1999.
73 *The World is Not Enough.* 1999.

herself and is ready to sleep with him parallels the changes in society.

It's no longer acceptable to lay a casual peck on the cheek in the workplace, but after Bond has earned a woman's affection, he can still make a few sex puns. Clearly, Dr. Jones is receptive to his jokes, maybe even finding them funny. If she didn't, Jones probably would have slapped him.

Looking at this scene through that lens, this humor is pretty different. Obviously there's a line that should never be crossed, as demeaning a woman is never acceptable, but the series is conveying the idea Bond needs consent before engaging in raunchy behavior.

That's true for every man in the 21st century. An innocent, corny sex joke on the 10th date is going to go over a lot better with the average lady than on the first date.

Still, the most drastic change to humor in the series occurred when Daniel Craig became Bond. That's because, at that point, the series turned its focus away from humor.

It's interesting to think about why the series chose to do this. As described earlier, Craig's Bond is the most serious and is supposedly a more accurate portrayal of the character from the Fleming novels.

In four films with Craig, there are less gadgets, less sex, and fewer to no puns. In general, the films have been less fun.

There are a lot of different possibilities as to why. For one, the Bond series seemed to realize that demeaning female names were no longer acceptable in society. Even puns about big female chests and other body parts weren't going to be usable either. That eliminated a lot of the puns.

In the early films, scenes with Bond and Q discussing the latest gadget technology led to a lot of humor, but that doesn't occur much with the new films. After *Die Another Day*, Q didn't return as a character until *Skyfall*, and even then, he was rebranded in a much different fashion.

With less casual sex too, there has been fewer opportunities for Craig's Bond to unleash a funny one-liner. But even after kills, which Craig's Bond has done plenty of, he typically hasn't stated anything noteworthy either.

While this could be a way the series is returning to its roots and to the original character, this change seems to be more than that. It's more than avoiding controversial sexual scenes too.

Starting in the mid-2000's, Hollywood began making action films with more realism. The best examples are probably through the endless new-aged superhero movies that started with *X-Men* in 2000 and really grew in popularity with *Batman Begins* in 2005.

Yes, these films are based on comic book heroes, and in that sense, there's not much realism to them. However, the direction of the films made the stories more relatable to everyday audiences. Gone were Tim Burton's comic-book feel movies and Joel Schumacher's nipple-suited Batman, and here was a seemingly more authentic version of the superhero.

It was hardly the film's only issue, but the audience's thirst for more realism was part of why *Batman and Robin* did so poorly.

From *The Atlantic*:

"Schumacher (the movie's director) had made a film that leaned even further into the campy 1960s tone of Adam West's *Batman* at a time when audiences were craving something more serious."[74]

There's plenty still in the Bond series that isn't realistic, but the over-the-top parts of the series -- the invisible car, other decadent gadgets, obvious sexual puns -- aren't part of 007 in the 21st century.

The depiction of masculinity in the newer films plays a role in this too. Again, Craig's Bond is more vulnerable. He doesn't need to make a wise crack in the face of danger like the previous actors who played the role.

Craig isn't always dreary, and as viewers saw in the exchange between Bond and Lynd when he awoke after the torture scene in *Casino Royale*, Bond still engages in the occasional double entendre. But usually, his sense of humor showcases his bitterness more than anything else.

Bond: [at a bar] Vodka martini.

Bartender: Shaken or stirred?

Bond: Do I look like I give a damn?[75]

---

[74] David Sims, "How *Batman & Robin* Changed the Superhero Movie for the Better," *The Atlantic*, June 20, 2017, https://www.theatlantic.com/entertainment/archive/2017/06/batman-and-robin-20th-anniversary/530997/.
[75] *Casino Royale*. 2006.

By Craig's fourth installment, *Spectre*, 007 is more comical, but not because of one-liners, and very rarely are any of the jokes sexual.

Clinic Barman: Can I get you something, sir?

Bond: Vodka martini. Shaken, not stirred.

Clinic Barman: I'm sorry, we don't serve alcohol.

Bond: [with obvious sarcasm] I'm already starting to love this place …

Craig's funniest line as Bond came next:

Clinic Barman: Here you are, sir. One Proteolytic digestive enzyme shake.

Bond: Do me a favor, will you? Throw that down the toilet. Cut out the middleman.[76]

There are other humorous scenes in *Spectre*. For example, when Bond is hanging on to a collapsing building and then falls several stories, he manages to comfortably land on a couch. There's another comedic scene when he can't use the gun on his car because Q didn't load the bullets. Furthermore, the scene where he threatens a tiny mouse with his Walther PPK saying, "Who do you work for?" produces some laughs too.

After his train battle with Hinx (Dave Bautista), Bond and Dr. Swann are exhausted and out of breath from the fighting. Swann turns to Bond and asks, "What do we do now?"[77]

---

[76] *Spectre*. 2015.
[77] *Spectre*. 2015.

Fittingly, the very next shot is of Bond and Swann entering their room, kissing and removing clothing as they head to the bed.

These moments are comical not to the point of being cheesy like in the 1970's, but they are self-reflexive. Rather than Bond being inexplicably uninjured after falling several feet and hitting concrete like in other films, Craig's Bond is saved by a random couch. Both situations are unrealistic, but the latter is poking a little fun at the action genre.

Just like these scenes, Craig's dialogue helps soften the violence, which is at an all-time high in the series during the 21st century. His dialogue just doesn't follow the same formula for humor from early in the series.

Craig's Bond isn't as cool as the others, but he gives audiences a more accurate portrayal of a spy. The change in the way the films use humor has helped the series continue to resonate to a new, less sex-driven, more realism-seeking generation.

6

"WE HAD SOME TROUBLE AT THE AIRPORT"

While critics have sometimes harshly judged the way in which the series portrayed women and sexuality in the 1960's and 1970's, the same cannot be said for race. Even today, there's not the same outcry about Bond being racist as there is for him being a misogynist.

The Bond character himself is not racist, but if fans placed the depiction of race early in the 007 films under the same critical microscope as sexuality, one could conclude the series has been even more racist than sexist.

But it's not as though the series is blatantly racist (in most cases, it's not), rather some of the films poorly display particular groups of people, leading to terrible stereotypes. Interestingly, Asians, and not black people, received the worst treatment among all the races in the series during the 1960's.

The first film's antagonist, Dr. Julius No (Joseph Wiseman), is half Chinese and half German. Sure, his half Chinese heritage gives the early 1960's film some diversity, but Dr. No is a brilliant nuclear physicist for Spectre. Making this character even half Chinese plays into the stereotype -- which Asians continue to battle in modern day -- that all Asians are smart and good at science and math.

This is hardly the only time the series portrays this stereotype. In *Goldfinger*, the scientist Goldfinger hires to install a radiological weapon is also Asian. In fact, all of Goldfinger's army and Oddjob are of Asian descent.

Why? This makes no sense. Goldfinger is white, and the film doesn't suggest he has any Asian connections. The closest region depicted in the film to an Asian country is Geneva, which is in central Europe.

This makes the inclusion of Asian characters nonsensical. It's as if the film purposefully showcases Asians as evil, and again, smart, villainess scientists.

Fortunately, the series begins to depict more diversity with Asians starting with *You Only Live Twice*. Rather than small parts as scientists and henchmen, Japanese actors and actresses received much bigger roles. Tetsurô Tanba played Tiger Tanaka, who is the head of the Japanese Secret Service, and Akiko Wakabayashi portrayed Aki, who, again, is the first female secret agent in the series and the first Asian Bond girl.

Still, there are major race issues with the film. Most of the movie takes place in Japan, and the film depicts the country as very primitive. Rather than fancy hotels, casinos and the best restaurants, Bond is treated to a sumo wrestling match and shares a bath with Tanaka, where multiple women wearing nothing but underwear wash both men.

Tanaka: My friend, now you take your first civilized bath.

Bond: Really?

[Bond is surrounded by four young Japanese women wearing only white bras and panties].

Bond: Oh, I like the plumbing.

Tanaka: Place yourself entirely in their hands, my dear Bond-san. Rule No. 1 is never do anything for yourself when someone else can do it for you.

Bond: And number two?

Tanaka: Rule No. 2 - in Japan, men always come first, women come second.

Bond: I might just retire to here [heads to bath tub with a woman].[78]

This monologue could easily be labeled sexist, but the fact it's taking place in Japan makes it also problematic with race. While maybe this was mostly true at that time, the film has an undertone meaning that Japan isn't as stylish or avant-garde as England, the United States and the rest of western society.

Instead, it seems to portray Japan the way most Americans already view the country. It's no different than if a Japanese film characterized the United States filled with overweight people eating burgers, hot dogs, chicken wings and fries while screaming at the television over an American football game. It's a stereotype that is far from always true.

---

[78] *You Only Live Twice.* 1967.

Bond also meets local MI6 operative Dikko Henderson (Charles Gray) while in Tokyo in *You Only Live Twice*. Having lived in Japan for 28 years, Henderson greets Bond wearing a kimono and then takes him through his Japanese-looking (it has sliding doors and wooden engawa verandas) house. This is another example of how the film plays right into Japanese stereotypes.

The same can mostly be said about *The Man with the Golden Gun*. In this film, Bond visits Beirut, Hong Kong, and Bangkok, none of which really receive the same elegant treatment as a western city. Bond at least stays in an extravagant hotel in Hong Kong and Bangkok, but in Hong Kong, he spends a night at a strip joint called Bottoms Up Club.

While Bottoms Up Club is actually a real club in Hong Kong, the realism doesn't hide the fact that the series still didn't depict Asian cities positively. When he's in western cities, Bond's adventures never take him to a strip club.

In Bangkok, Bond meets the film's villain, Scaramanga, at a Muay Thai event, which is Thai boxing -- close to modern-day UFC. This isn't explained in any dialogue, though, and the viewer could mistakenly believe the series has once again taken Bond to another sumo wrestling match.

Prior to that scene, different sumo wrestlers capture Bond and place him in a martial arts academy. Again, these are more examples of Asian stereotypes, and the Austin Power series pokes fun at the reoccurring sumo wrestling scenes of the Bond films with the Fat Bastard character.

The use of Nick Nack (Hervé Villechaize), who is Scaramanga's manservant with dwarfism, in the film is peculiar as well. After

Bond foils Scaramanga's plans and destroys his estate, Nick Nack attacks Bond and Goodnight in an act of revenge. Bond doesn't have much trouble beating him in a fight, though, and stuffs the little person in a suitcase.

Clearly, the series didn't hold the dwarf community in very high regard in 1974. This connects to a pattern not necessarily pertaining to race but to how the series portrays people who are different. Early in the series, the films display villains without hands and arms, as dwarfs and giants (Jaws in *The Spy Who Loved Me* and *Moonraker*), and with scars.

This comes back to the idea of Bond's physique. Bond is the ultimate good-looking white man, and the series conveys that with contrasting villains, who look different from an everyday person. Where applicable, the early part of the series uses race in the same manner -- expressing the message that diverging from white European is somehow villainous.

That's certainly how black people seem to be portrayed in *Live and Let Die*. In the 1960's, the series didn't portray them as poorly as Asians, but then again, there were barely any black characters. In *Dr. No*, Bond's boat driver, Quarrel (John Kitzmiller), and the villain's henchmen, the Three Blind Mice (Eric Coverly, Charles Edghill, Henry Lopez), are the only black people in the film and are killed. The only real notable thing about Quarrel is he wears a ridiculously bright red shirt despite the fact they are supposed to be undercover.

There isn't another significant black character for nine more years. But while *Live and Let Die* definitely had more diversity, there are massive racist undertones.

Georgia State University PHD student Jacqueline Ristola ripped the film to shreds, calling it "a blaxploitation film" and "the worst entry of the franchise."

> It is a film that does not empower African Americans, but rather regurgitates blaxploitation tropes without their original empowering subtext. The film instead reduces the tropes to their most racist form, parading them as a form of cultural tourism Bond undergoes as he traverses the seedy lands of blaxploitation. Pimps, drugs, Voodoo; Bond encounters them all. What results is racist exploitation of blaxploitation iconography within the film, creating an onslaught of reductionistic, racist imagery.[79]

Ristola also argued Bond's character embodies British imperialism in the film. With that in mind, she reads 007 rescuing Solitaire, the Bond girl of the story, from African-American gangsters, as the film conveying the idea that being associated with "British imperialism and whiteness is better than being with black men any day."[80]

Ristola conceives this argument with the notion that her audience has also read the book. As I mentioned in the introduction, my theories only focus on the Bond films, and primarily on the canon 007 movies.

Without the context from the novel, it's probably a stretch to say Bond embodies British imperialism, but there's still a lot of

[79] Jacqueline Ristola, "Racist Cultural Appropriation in *Live and Let Die*," *Media Commons*, November, 12, 2015, http://mediacommons.org/imr/2015/10/28/racist-cultural-appropriation-live-and-let-die.
[80] Ristola "Racist Cultural Appropriation in *Live and Let* Die."

merit to the rest of Ristola's argument. Similar to *You Only Live Twice*, *Live and Let Die* relies heavily upon black stereotypes that will entertain a primarily white, American and British audience.

The film displays black people as pimps and primitive voodoo believers with afros. Just like with the Dr. No character, who is half Asian and a nuclear scientist, Dr. Kananga, the antagonist of *Live and Let Die*, is black and a drug dealer, playing into terrible stereotypes that both races still battle against today. Coincidentally, Kananga's sidekick, Tee Hee (Julius Harris), who's also black, is missing an arm. Dr. No has no hands, and the lack of limbs leads to both of their demises in each film.

Live and Let Die is the eighth Bond film, and in the previous seven, every villain is at least half white and desires world domination. But Kananga, the first black villain, only wishes to deal heroin. One could argue this fact alone supports Ristola's claim that the film fails to empower the African-American race.

The only significant black character painted in a positive light is Rosie Carver (Gloria Hendry), who is a rogue CIA agent. Before discovering that Kananga sent her to kill Bond, 007 sleeps with her. While this is Bond's first sexual encounter with a black woman in the series, that's the extent of the film revolutionizing race relations between white and black. Carver is depicted as a terrible agent, and she meets her death shortly after experiencing Bond's skills.

Though it's not as if *Live and Let Die* does a better job of avoiding stereotypes with white people either. Sheriff Pepper (Clifton James), who is involved in the film's famous bayou boat chase, works as a representation of white southerners. While his character is mostly used to add humor, he plays right into the stereotypical portrayal of dumb, simple, arrogant southerners.

What's worse, the series uses Sheriff Pepper again in the next film *The Man with the Golden Gun*. Despite making little sense, Bond runs into Pepper while chasing Scaramanga in Bangkok - - that's apparently where Pepper, a police officer from Louisiana, goes on vacation.

Fortunately, the series transitioned away from its prejudice rhetoric much faster than it did for the gender inequality issues. That's probably the biggest reason why race isn't something often discussed with the Bond series while sexism certainly is.

With *Moonraker*, the series had a major breakthrough on the race front. The film's antagonist, Drax (Michael Lonsdale), has an evil scheme to create a "new master race." Drax plans to destroy human life by launching nerve gas onto Earth. Then, once it's safe, repopulate Earth with the descendants of his hand-picked genetically perfected young men and women aboard his spaceship.

His genetically-perfect humans are supposed to be of all races, but most of the ones shown on screen are white. Even so, no audience member in 1979 heard the term "master race" in the movie and didn't immediately think of Adolf Hitler.

The film's use of the term makes it obvious Bond is fighting for social injustice, giving *Moonraker* one of the series' early political statements.

Then in the 1980's, the series seemed to make a conscience effort to keep the villains Eastern European. In *Octopussy*, Bond visits India for the first time, so that opens opportunities for a new group of people, but the main characters stay mostly white with the exception of top henchman Gobinda (Kabir Bedi) and Bond's Indian contact, Vijay (Vijay Amritraj). Gobinda is an underrated sidekick villain in the series. He wears a turban, but it isn't done distastefully. Vijay is a likeable character too, but he meets his death too early in the film.

However, that doesn't mean the series was free of all racism. The film could have done without this line.

> Bond: [after handing a wad of Indian cash to his accomplice] That should keep you in curry for a few weeks.[81]

Similar to the way *You Only Live Twice* and *The Man with the Golden Gun* did with Asian countries, *Octopussy* plays to the stereotypes westerners may possess of India in certain scenes. But perhaps one small improvement was in the fact India isn't portrayed as primitive as other Asian countries were in the 1960's and 1970's.

By 1985, the series was ready for 007 to sleep with another black woman. Her name is May Day (Grace Jones), and in *A View to a Kill*, she is the femme fatale of the film. After Max Zorin (Christopher Walken) betrays her, May Day redeems herself by helping Bond defeat Zorin.

In the process, though, May Day is killed in an explosion, which continued a troubling trend of non-white characters meeting their death in the series. Bond has slept with three black women in 24 films, and only one lived.

---

[81] *Octopussy*. Directed by John Glen. 1983. Beverly Hills, CA: MGM/United Artists, DVD.

Still, when compared to other action films of the mid-1980's, Bond was probably ahead of its time with the May Day character. Indiana Jones, Star Wars and other popular action series didn't have their white action heroes sleeping with black women. Most of the time, they didn't have any major black characters either.

Witness, another film starring Harrison Ford, received an Oscar nomination for Best Picture in 1985. It's a beautiful story about how love sometimes isn't enough to keep two people together. John Book (Ford) and Rachel Lapp (Kelly McGillis) fall in love with each other, but Book is a cop from Philadelphia, and Lapp is Amish. Their different backgrounds keep them from living happily ever after.

This is a story a mixed-race couple would most obviously connect to, and yet, there are barely any non-white characters. Plus, the two main black characters in the film are both killed.

So while the Bond series certainly had its lack of diversity issues and the troubling trend of killing off non-white characters, other Hollywood films had this problem before the 1990's too, especially films in the horror genre.[82] The series continued to attempt better racial depictions at the end of the 1980's, but major issues persisted.

In 1987, the Bond series, though, was about as forward thinking as anybody could imagine with one particular line. In *The Living Daylights*, 007 befriends Kamran Shah (Art Malik), who is Deputy Commander of the Afghan Mujaheddin's Eastern

---

[82] "The Black Death: A Brief History of Black People Dying in Horror Movies," *Black Horror Movies*, April 18, 2019, http://www.blackhorrormovies.com/blackdeath/.

District during the Soviet-Afghan War. At the end of the film, Shah and his men arrive late to see Kara Milovy's solo cellist performance. The exchange was probably supposed to be just one final attempt to give the audience a laugh, but it's rather eerie watching it today.

> Shah: [holding Kara's hand] I'm sorry we missed the concert. We had some trouble at the airport.

> M: [sarcastically] Can't imagine why.[83]

It's impossible to watch this scene today without 21st century context, in which Middle Eastern-looking people are generally the ones that have the hardest times at airport security in western society. This exchange isn't inherently racist, but rather makes light of racism that already exists. In that sense, it's rather forward-thinking and is still relevant in the modern era.

The scene, though, isn't completely revolutionary. The Afghan men enter the black-tie event in the same clothes they wore into battle, and two of them are even still wearing their bullet belts.

Either this is all part of the joke -- M's line working as a reminder that, "of course you had trouble at the airport, you basically brought your AK-47's with you" -- or the film simply failed to paint these Afghan characters as anything but violent, war-time fighters, stereotyping yet another group.

The series runs into the stereotyping problem again in *License to Kill*. In Dalton's last adventure as Bond, 007 battles a Central American criminal cartel. Similar to the way the series portrays black people in *Live and Let Die*, the series depicts Spanish-

---

[83] *The Living Daylights*. 1987.

speaking people in *License to Kill* as criminal cartel mongrels and drug dealers, playing to yet another stereotype of the late 1980's.

To this day, there hasn't been another Bond film to feature Hispanic or Latino people. However, the series began a movement to become much more diverse in 1997.

M's top aide and Deputy Chief of Staff, Charles Robinson, is played by black actor Colin Salmon. He was the strong-silent type, as he didn't receive many lines, but he makes appearances in three films and diehard Bond fans know him.

Also in 1997, the series redeems itself with much better depictions of Asia in *Tomorrow Never Dies*. A lot of that is done through Chinese secret agent Wai Lin, who helps Bond stop Elliot Carver's evil plan.

Bond sleeps with his third black woman, Jinx, during *Die Another Day*, and this one lives. North Koreans serve as the primary villains in the film, but because of gene technology, the North Korean People's Army Colonel, Tan-Sun Moon (Will Yun Lee), becomes Gustav Graves (Toby Stephens). At least in appearance to the audience, the villain evolves into a white man.

The series has developed more black characters in the latest edition of the series. In *Casino Royale*, Bond's long-time friend and co-worker, American CIA agent Felix Leiter, is played by a black actor (Jeffrey Wright).

Leiter is black in *Never Say Never Again* (1983) as well, but that film is a remake of *Thunderball* and is not part of the original Bond canon. So a black actor playing Leiter in 2006 was a big deal. Moneypenny also becomes black when the character returns with Naomie Harris in the role during *Skyfall*.

Whenever possible, the series now inserts characters of different races. At the poker table in *Casino Royale*, the only other featured characters besides Bond and Le Chiffre are black and Asian.

But despite this desire for more diversity, the series continues to resist making the villains anything but European. In *Skyfall* and *Spectre*, not only are the villains white, they are also British, helping to indicate the idea that in the modern world, western society's enemies are domestic as well as foreign.

In this post-September 11th era, the series could easily make Muslim-looking characters villains or evil terrorists, but the films have rightfully strayed from making that stereotype. They've stayed away from it so much that the series may be making the political statement that white people can be terrorists as evil, conniving and villainous as any group.

Fewer stereotypes and more diversity both led to a greater product. It also led to three other essential changes for the series -- a feeling of modernization, another level of realism and an appeal to a wider audience. The more the series can satisfy these three goals, the easier it will be to continue remaining popular well into the 21st century.

7

"THIS NEVER HAPPENED TO THE OTHER FELLOW"

One of the coolest things about Bond is he never ages. He's been a spy in his thirties for almost six decades.

Yet, technology, culture and society move forward.

If one laid out a timeline of the first 20 Bond films, it wouldn't make sense. Bond couldn't possibly appear to be 30 years old when most of his missions involve the Cold War and then still look the same age in a film that clearly takes place after the fall of the Soviet Union.

But early on and even into the early 2000's, this didn't seem to matter. Audiences just accepted that Bond -- both the series and the character -- was timeless.

However, that changed when viewers responded well to action films featuring more authenticity and realism.[84] With this adjusted attitude, Bond needed to be vulnerable, and he had to

---

[84] Laura Rosenfeld, "5 Ways 'Batman Begins' Changed Hollywood Forever," *Tech Times*, June 15, 2015, https://www.techtimes.com/articles/58219/20150615/how-batman-begins-changed-hollywood-forever.htm.

be a colder killer, yet a more sympathetic lover. On top of that, audiences wanted a reason for why he never ages.

Thus, the Bond codename theory was born.

The theory states that James Bond isn't actually the spy's real name, but a name the MI6 gives agents once they reach double-0 status. With this theory, the name James Bond works exactly as the 007 code. It's an identification the agent will only use while he is employed as a secret agent at MI6. Upon retirement, according to the theory, the agent will return to his birth name.

So, with each new actor that plays Bond, the audience is not just seeing a new actor, they are witnessing a new agent rising the ranks, becoming 007 and taking on the codename -- James Bond. This not only explains why he doesn't age, but also why each actor has a different portrayal of the character -- because they are actually playing a different person -- a different James Bond.

There's plenty of proof in the series that gives this theory merit. The first supporting evidence actually happens in *On Her Majesty's Secret Service* in George Lazenby's very first scene as Bond.

A woman, who the audience later learns is Tracy di Vicenzo, passes Bond driving along the coast of Portugal and then stops to take a walk on the beach. Bond spies on her and discovers she plans to commit suicide by walking into the ocean. 007 runs to save her, which he successfully does, but before he can begin working his charm, two henchmen attack Bond and di Vicenzo, separating the two of them.

Bond defeats them both, but di Vicenzo drives away. At the end of the scene, Lazenby's Bond looks into the camera and says, "this never happened to the other fellow."[85]

The "other fellow" he's referring to is, of course, Sean Connery. It's a joke on the fact that in his very first scene as Bond, Lazenby doesn't attract the woman while Connery (or the writers of the first five films) never let a beautiful woman slip away.

For those unaware, this action -- where actors speak directly to the audience -- is called "breaking the fourth wall."[86] Lazenby talking straight into the camera is his way of admitting that "this is a film, and I'm playing a role that some other fellow used to." It's the only instance in the Bond canon where the fourth wall is violated.

It's a funny one-liner, perhaps Lazenby's best of the film, and that's it. That's probably it's only intention.

But believers of the Bond codename theory could use this as their first evidence. Connery and Lazenby's Bond characters are different people -- he admitted so in this scene.

The other strong supporting evidence to this theory is the way in which the series replaces actors as other characters who keep the same name. Four different actors have played the leader of MI6, and all four went by M. With each transition to the next

---

85 *On Her Majesty's Secret Service. Directed by Peter R. Hunt.* 1969. Beverly Hills, CA: United Artists, DVD.
86 https://alwaysactingup.wordpress.com/what-is-the-4th-wall/.

M, the series left clues that the new M is, in fact, a different person.

Bernard Lee plays M through the first 11 films. Lee died in 1981 before the filming of *For Your Eyes Only* began, and out of respect to Lee, the series didn't replace his character with a new actor immediately, instead explaining in the 1981 film that M was on leave.[87] Then Robert Brown assumed the role of M in *Octopussy*.

However, Brown played a small role, Admiral Hargreaves, in *The Spy Who Loved Me*. So with Brown becoming M three films later, the hot-button question is did Admiral Hargreaves become the new MI6 leader and thus take on the codename M? Or, is Brown simply playing the same M that Lee did for the greater part of two decades?

While there's no clear-cut answer, at least the question of whether or not M is a codename is answered in *Goldeneye* when Judi Dench assumes the role. Dench obviously can't be the same M from the first 16 films because of her sex, and therefore, the series is suggesting that M is a codename transferred down to each new MI6 leader.

Most certainly, this is the case when Dench's M ends her tenure, which unfortunately happens when she dies at the end of *Skyfall*. Upon her death, the Chairman of the Intelligence and Security Committee, Gareth Mallory (Ralph Fiennes), who fights for the continued existence of MI6 throughout the film, assumes the leadership role of MI6. At the very end of the film,

---

[87] Pfeiffer, Lee; Worrall, Dave (1998). *The essential Bond*. London: Boxtree Ltd.

Bond calls him "M" thus absolutely confirming M is a codename passed down from person to person.

Q works in the same manner. The original Q (Desmond Llewelyn) serves as Bond's go-to gadget man for 19 films, but in *The World is Not Enough*, he retires, giving way to his successor, played by John Cleese. Bond jokingly calls Cleese's character "R" when he first meets him, but in the next film, *Die Another Day*, Cleese plays the same character, who is now referred to as "Q."

Just like the MI6 leader will be called "M", the British Secret Service's technology department's leader will assume the codename "Q."

The last name the series reuses is the aforementioned Quarrel, who is Bond's black boat driver in *Dr. No*. Again, viewers probably remember him as the man wearing a red shirt while undercover, who meets his demise via a machine-built dragon.

While aboard a boat in *Live and Let Die*, Bond mentions to Rosie Carver that his boat driver's name is Quarrel Jr. (Roy Stewart), meaning the son of the original Quarrel from a decade earlier.

This is important for two reasons. It's possible the filmmakers reused the Quarrel name only to pay homage to the series' original story. It's one of the first instances of nostalgia in the series, which is a topic discussed at length in the next chapter.

There is no mention of Quarrel having a son in the series' first film, but the fact Quarrel Jr. in *Live and Let Die* is presumably about the same age that his father was in *Dr. No* indicates at least some passage of time. Yet Bond appears to be the same age. Hypothetically, couldn't the name James Bond work in the same fashion as M and Q, thus explaining why Quarrel Jr. is an adult?

It's definitely possible, but there is also evidence to suggest the Bond codename theory is not true, and that each actor who plays him is still portraying the same person.

The most obvious evidence is Bond's marriage in *On Her Majesty's Secret Service*. Lazenby's Bond marries di Vicenzo, and yet, with Moore's Bond in *The Spy Who Loved Me*, Amasova brings up the fact his wife had been killed (this scene is referenced in Chapter 1). In that scene, Bond is very sensitive to this fact, and he remains so whenever someone mentions marriage to him in subsequent films.

In *License to Kill*, CIA agent Felix Leiter (David Hedison) marries at the beginning of the film, and his new wife, Della (Priscilla Barnes) throws her garter at Bond in a playful manner after all the other guests have left the reception. She's implying to Bond that he will be the next to get married. Bond doesn't like the joke, though, and he says goodnight. Leiter then explains to his new wife that Bond was married once but a long time ago.

Then in *The World is Not Enough*, Elektra King hits upon the touchy subject again.

> King: Tell me, have you ever lost a loved one, Mr. Bond?

> Bond: [hesitant in his answer] M sent me because we're afraid your life might be in danger.[88]

---

[88] *The World is Not Enough*. 1999.

During his hesitation, Bond squirms a bit. Clearly, King hit a nerve, and the series seems to be implying it's because Bond still does love his dead wife.

These three scenes connect Moore, Dalton and Brosnan's Bonds to Lazenby's in 1969. Of course, Bond codename theory believers would make the counterargument that just because each actor's version of Bond is spooked by the mention of marriage or the loss of true love doesn't automatically mean they are the same person. For Moore and Dalton's Bonds, it could just be a coincidence, as they could have also been married to different women and lost their wives.

The King-Bond scene is even more vague. Bond could be affected by her question because he grew up an orphan due to the loss of his parents.

However, that doesn't explain Moore's Bond visiting his wife's grave in the first scene of *For Your Eyes Only*. Bond places flowers in front of a tombstone, which clearly reads:

Teresa Bond
1943-1969
Beloved wife of James Bond
"We have all the time in the World"

If James Bond was only a codename, then Teresa wouldn't have taken Bond as her last name upon marrying 007. The inclusion of the years and the slogan at the bottom also eliminate the possibility that it's a different Teresa. This is the same woman who suffered death at the hands of Blofeld in the final scene of *On Her Majesty's Secret Service*, which hit theaters in 1969.

So, at the very least, Moore and Lazenby's 007 are the same person. At the beginning of *Diamonds Are Forever*, Connery is back as Bond and tracking down Blofeld as if he needs to kill him for revenge. Maybe the early Connery Bond is a different person, but the Bond that Connery plays in *Diamonds Are Forever* seems to be the same as Lazenby and thus would also be the same as Moore's 007.

Craig's Bond may be the same as well for a very similar reason. In *Skyfall*, he returns to his childhood house, where his parent's tombstone reads, "Andrew Bond and Monique Delacroix Bond." Again, if Bond were a codename, his mother and father wouldn't have the same last name.

Still, that hasn't stopped fans from producing other theories explaining why the Bond codename theory exists. Minneapolis-based blogger and writer D.F. Lovett argued in February 2015 that Bond could still be a codename despite both tombstones:

> What I suggest instead is this: James Bond is a codename, but James Bond doesn't know that it's a codename. Why? Because the man who knows himself as James Bond has been brainwashed.
>
> The suggestions of this reality are all there, with one standing above all the others: the relationship between Raoul Silva (Javier Bardem's character), M (Judi Dench), and James Bond. Silva is a former MI6 agent who worked under M, before taking up the occupation of cyber-terrorist. Throughout the film, he repeatedly attempts to bond with 007, including referring to both himself and Bond as rats, held and tortured by M.

And this next part of my theory is a credit to Bardem's acting, as it's something I cannot capture through simple plot synopsis and analysis. There is an element to Bardem's acting that not only ensnares you, but in which it appears that he has a secret he isn't sharing. His grin, his eyes, his body language, and the way he lingers on certain words as he speaks.[89]

All the sudden, our fun and simple "good versus evil" action series just got *really* complicated.

Bloomberg columnist Stephen L. Carter has his own theory, writing in 2013 that Silva is actually M's long-lost son.[90] But that doesn't mean he's her biological son; Lovett argued Silva is just one of her many former agents.

> My interpretation is not that he is the literal son of M, but that he identifies as one of her many sons, as all her agents are her sons. But he is also this: the only other living James Bond.

> It explains his connection (and affection) regarding Bond, his disdain for M, their complicated dynamic, and, finally, let's return to Bardem's acting. Remember that knowing look of his? It's on full view as he arrives at Skyfall, casually walking out of his helicopter and tossing grenades at the

---

[89] D.F. Lovett, "Yes, Indeed, James Bond is a Codename (And Skyfall Proved it)," What Would Bale Do, February 24, 2015, https://whatwouldbaledo.com/2015/02/24/yes-indeed-james-bond-is-a-codename/.

[90] Stephen L. Carter, "The Secret James Bond Missed in 'Skyfall,'" Bloomberg, November 11, 2013, https://www.bloomberg.com/opinion/articles/2013-11-11/the-secret-james-bond-missed-in-skyfall-.

house. He remembers Skyfall well. It's the place he had been brainwashed into believing was his childhood home. Just as Daniel Craig's Bond was brainwashed into thinking the same thing. The brainwashing was so thorough, the identity so complete, that Silva even knew Bond would bring M there, and he had prepared for it. Not only is it the place where they are brainwashed into believing they were raised, but it is also the place where their training and brainwashing occurred.[91]

Lovett also contends that this explains the tombstones and the small connections each Bond has to the others. Growing up as an orphan, 007 was brainwashed with the same memories -- losing his wife, the other missions, etc. -- as the other Bonds.

Lovett makes a lot of interesting points, and he supports his argument well, but to be clear, this is not a theory I believe. It's fascinating to think about the possibility, and perhaps the filmmakers left tiny clues to leave a door to this theory cracked just a smidge for huge fans to open. In recent years, the Bond series has been extremely self aware, which is another topic we'll discuss later.

But there are counterpoints to be made with this theory as well. If Bond simply comes from an assembly line of brainwashed orphans who are raised to be cold-hearted killers, why hasn't M replaced 007 after he is presumed dead in *Skyfall*? Furthermore, when M writes his obituary, she used Bond as his name, indicating it's not a codename.

---

[91] Lovett "Yes, Indeed."

For what it's worth, my opinion is there can be a combination of these two sides. For the most part, yours truly would argue James Bond is the birth name of one man, and the producers keep him ageless in an effort to keep the films contemporary.

However, Craig's Bond is different in some form or fashion.

Casino Royale works as a way to display to audiences how Bond becomes 007. In the first scene, Bond kills two men, which was his last task to earning his double-0 status. It's also quite clear that he's on his first mission throughout the film, and he has not yet grown attached to certain items as the other Bonds.

As mentioned in Chapter 5, Craig's Bond doesn't order his vodka martini shaken, not stirred. This line is supposed to function as humor -- a parody of the previous films -- but it also reveals how Bond becomes who he is throughout the rest of the series. Presumably, the bartender makes his vodka martini shaken, not stirred in this scene. Bond likes it and then orders it that way from that point forward.

The Dutch-Scratching scene serves a similar purpose, as it explains why Bond can have sex with multiple women in every film, and yet he never impregnates one. His broken heart over Vesper Lynd also shows why he never truly trusts another woman again.

In this sense, *Casino Royale* is a prequel -- the film shows how Bond becomes the 007 who audiences had been watching (at that point) for more than four decades. And yet, the film is set in modern times, so there's no possible way it could be a true prequel.

With the release of *Spectre*, Craig's Bond feels more like a remake than a prequel. 007's arch nemesis, Ernst Blofeld, returns even though he's been dead for years, and the film reveals that he's been the villainous mastermind behind every plot to destroy Craig's Bond. Waltz's Blofeld is first shown with an unblemished face, but then Swann throws Bond's exploding watch at him in order to escape. As a result, Blofeld gets the circular scar around his eye, which he was famous for in *You Only Live Twice*.

Even if the codename theory is true, and Craig's Bond has undergone massive brainwashing, that doesn't explain the reappearance of Blofeld in *Spectre*. Blofeld should be 50 years older too, so why isn't he?

For these reasons, Craig's Bond can't be described as a prequel or a remake but rather a "reboot" of the series. There are instances of similarities that make the films with Craig feel like remakes, but they stand alone. In essence, it's returning the series to what's familiar to its fans, and in that way, it's no different than the new *Star Wars* films, which are even closer to remakes of the originals, except the characters have aged.

Re-inserting Blofeld is no different than the Batman series rebranding the Joker in *The Dark Knight* even though Jack Nicholson's version of the villain fell to his death in 1989.

Craig's Bond is the same 007, but he exists in a different timeline or in an alternative universe from the original Bond. They exist -- in movie form -- side-by-side, which allows the series to continue with the same character in contemporary times.

Just giving fans the possibility of the Bond codename theory has helped the series stay current. It gives the audience striving for authenticity a more realistic explanation for why he never ages. The series provides plenty of evidence for the contrary as well for the viewers who remain steadfast that there is only one 007.

At the end of the day, each individual viewer can decide which theory they believe is right. Really, that's become part of the fun in the series. It's not about having the right answer -- the codename theory gives viewers a compelling and entertaining debate.

8

"SOMETIMES THE OLD WAYS ARE THE BEST"

Even for a series that's lasted more than five decades, storytelling remains vitally important. That's the biggest reason why the series nearly died in the late 1980's -- the plot lines of a few consecutive Bond films weren't very good.

But a film series also can't survive completely on good storytelling. As we've seen with a lot of older film series, invoking a strong sense of nostalgia has been key to keeping fans and making new ones in a second and third generation.

Creating nostalgia allows a series to showcase to the older fans that they haven't forgotten why the original films were so popular while also connecting the younger generation to those older movies.

If an adolescent had seen *Goldfinger* before *Die Another Day*, he/she would understand the film's joke when Bond and Q (John Cleese) have this exchange in 2002.

Bond: You must be joking.

Q: As I learned from my predecessor, Bond, I never joke about my work.[92]

Connery's Bond and the original Q, played by Desmond Llewelyn, have the same exchange, which became the most famous Q moment of the series, almost 40 years earlier.

Bond: Ejector seat? You're joking.

Q: I never joke about my work, 007.[93]

It's references like these that give audiences reasons to continue watching the older films. There are small random examples of these kinds of references early in the series (such as the reuse of Quarrel's name in *Live and Let Die*), but the Bond films really started inserting subtle moments of nostalgia beginning with *Goldeneye*.

Throughout the film, Natalya Simonova continuously asks Bond why he seemingly destroys every vehicle he operates, which is comical not only because 007 struggles with moving vehicles in *Goldeneye*, but also in just about every other film in the series.

Then in the film's final scene after killing Alec Trevelyan and saving London from financial ruin, Bond and Simonova seem to be alone in a field. The film appears to be headed to the typical 007 movie ending -- an intimate, alone moment with a beautiful woman.

Not so fast this time.

---

[92] *Die Another Day*. 2002.
[93] *Goldfinger*. 1964.

Simonova: [while kissing Bond in a field] Suppose someone is watching.

Bond: There's no one within twenty-five miles, believe me.

[appearing out of nowhere] Jack Wade: Yo, Jimbo![94]

This isn't a full-blown nostalgic moment, but it does bring forth the memories the audience has of other endings in the series, and then it becomes comedic when Wade and his platoon of soldiers interrupt.

There's an even more subtle hint of nostalgia in *The World is Not Enough*. Towards the end of the film when Elektra King is about to begin torturing Bond in a garrote, King tells Bond she could have given him the world. Even close to his death, 007 keeps his cool and says:

Bond: The world is not enough.

King: Foolish sentiment.

Bond: Family motto.[95]

To the fan watching their first Bond film, it sounds like he's just being coy, but actually, this is a nod to *On Her Majesty's Secret Service*. 007 goes undercover in that film as a genealogist, and prior to his assignment, he researches his own family line. He finds his family crest and motto, which, in the film, is "the world is not enough."

---

[94] *Goldeneye*. 1995.
[95] *The World is Not Enough*. 1999.

(Sidebar: It also works as another way Brosnan's Bond and the previous 007's are connected as the same person, debunking the codename theory).

During the 1990's, the series becomes self-aware as well. In one of the first scenes with Judi Dench as M, she calls Bond a "sexist, misogynist dinosaur" and a "relic of the Cold War."[96] Oh, the irony, as a lot of 007 film critics have been calling the series "a relic of the Cold War" for the last two decades.

So not only have the series producers and writers been aware of the public's criticism for Bond over the last 20 years, they've addressed it with small changes. As argued in the second chapter, Bond is still a misogynist, but the series no longer accepts his behavior.

It's these types of strategies that helped the series rejuvenate itself following the end of the Cold War. Then, the series became very nostalgic in *Die Another Day*.

During the scene in which Q and Bond have the same exchange from *Goldfinger*, there are tons of "old relics" in the background. 007 passes the plane he flew and the alligator he used to go undercover in *Octopussy*. A knife also comes out of the front of a shoe -- a reference to *From Russia with Love*.

Then, Bond finds the jetpack he used in *Thunderball* and asks Q, "Does this still work?" Before he gets his invisible car, Q also gives Bond his latest gadget-filled watch.

Q: This will be your 20th, I believe.

---

[96] *Goldeneye*. 1995.

Bond: How time flies.

Q: Yes, well 007, why don't you establish a record by actually returning this one?[97]

Again, this obviously pays homage to the entire series, as *Die Another Day* was the 20th Bond film.

These were the most apparent instances of nostalgia in the movie, but there were other examples as well. The way Jinx walks out of the water and onto the beach is reminiscent of Honey Ryder from *Dr. No*. Jinx is even wearing the same type of bikini with a knife on her left belt buckle.

The plot structure of the film is also very similar to *Goldfinger*. Bond uses a Gustav Grave diamond as a way to meet the suspected villain. In *Goldfinger*, he uses a gold bar to meet Goldfinger, only this time, rather than playing golf, in *Die Another Day*, Bond fences.

These nearly identical plots are nothing new for the series. When Bond meets Kamal Khan (Louis Jourdan), the villain of *Octopussy*, he is cheating at backgammon, but 007 discovers this and embarrasses Khan just as he did when he learns Goldfinger is cheating at gin.

The series continues to be nostalgic and self-aware with Craig as 007 beginning in 2006. Again, M references yesteryear when Bond annoys her, saying "God, I miss the Cold War."

---

[97] *Die Another Day*. 2002.

Maybe they don't miss the Cold War itself, but upon hearing that line, a lot of the Bond audience probably thought, "Damn, I miss the 1970's and 1980's too."

As previously explained, *Casino Royale* works as a way for the series to show how Bond becomes 007 and the person he is. But his "do I look like I give a damn"[98] line to the bartender who asks him how he'd like his vodka martini is a reference to the "shaken, not stirred" line too. And when Bond walks out into the bathroom wearing his signature black-tie tuxedo, the audience can't help but feel reflective upon all the other films where he dons the tux beautifully.

Also in *Casino Royale*, the series inserts Bond himself into the "Honey Ryder" beach role. Wearing a ridiculously short bathing suit, 007 walks out of the water and onto the sand in much the same way Ryder and Jinx did in the previous films.

This showcases both nostalgia and self-awareness. Rather than continuing the sexist tradition of objectifying the women's bodies, this scene objectifies 007's assets. This signifies the series' willingness to change in order to bring on a bigger female audience.

An even more significant nostalgic moment occurs in *Quantum of Solace* when British secret service operative Strawberry Fields shows up dead with oil covering her body. In the scene, her dead body lays on the bed in the same fashion as Jill Masterson's in *Goldfinger*, only this time, it's oil instead of gold.

---

[98] *Casino Royale*. 2006.

As if that wasn't enough, upon discovering the body, the score plays a few familiar musical notes from the "Goldfinger" theme song. Anybody who saw *Goldfinger* before *Quantum of Solace* might have considered this scene one of the best in the new film.

However, there is such a thing as too much nostalgia. Because if there's excessive overlap between the old and new films -- it's worth wondering why even bother continuing to make new films (other than making money).

Walking this line is extremely important to maintaining a successful film franchise, and the series borders on featuring too many nostalgic moments during *Spectre*.

The opening scene of the film takes the audience to a Day of the Dead parade in Mexico City, which is reminiscent of the Mardi Gras parade in *Thunderball* and another festive parade Bond attends in *Moonraker*.

When the audience first sees Bond, he's wearing a skeleton mask, which is a nod to Baron Samurai in *Live and Let Die*. Then in the final 30 minutes of the film, there are repetitive references to 1960's Bond movies.

Bond and Madeleine Swann find Franz Oberhauser's secret lair in the Sahara Desert. The two of them are Oberhauser's guests just as Bond and Ryder were for Dr. No in the series' opening film. Oberhauser even leaves a kimono-looking dress on Swann's bed for her to wear, which looks awfully familiar to what Ryder wore to Dr. No's dinner.

Furthermore, Oberhauser wears the same villainous-looking, long-sleeved, shirt with the collar buttoned up like a turtleneck that has been featured throughout the series. And when Bond and Swann meet Oberhauser, they are admiring an asteroid he has collected just as 007 and Ryder were checking out the giant aquarium before meeting Dr. No.

Immediately after their introduction, the series then includes a new variation of the famous "Do you expect me to talk"[99] line from *Goldfinger*.

Oberhauser: So James, why did you come?

Bond: I came here to kill you.

Oberhauser: And I thought you came here to die.[100]

The nostalgia doesn't end there. After one of Oberhauser's henchmen knocks Bond unconscious, 007 awakens tied to a torture chair. As his eyesight becomes clearer, the camera shows a white cat similar to the one Blofeld had in many of the early 007 films.

Later in that scene, Oberhauser reveals that his father was the one who helped Bond when he first became an orphan. Growing jealous of the relationship his father and Bond created together, Oberhauser killed his father in an avalanche and staged his own death. After faking his death, Oberhauser changed his name to Ernst Stavro Blofeld.

Yes, Bond's original nemesis returns -- the one with whom most fans are familiar. Just the mention of his name brings back

---

[99] *Goldfinger*. 1964.
[100] *Spectre*. 2015.

memories to diehard fans, and then when Bond destroys his secret lair, Blofeld escapes but not without some damage.

In his next scene, Blofeld has the signature scar on his right eye. When the audience first sees Blofeld's face in *You Only Live Twice*, he has a similar scar on the same eye.

All of this works as a way to bring back those fond memories of 1960's Bond films. While it's mostly executed well, the series went a little overboard using all of these moments together. Not only is *Spectre* impossible to follow if one hasn't seen the other Craig films, it also isn't nearly as enjoyable if one hasn't also watched the Connery and Lazenby Bond adventures.

It would be better if the series found ways to insert nostalgic moments while still making each film stand alone. The predecessor of *Spectre*, *Skyfall*, did a better job of accomplishing this goal.

Similar to *Die Another Day*, *Skyfall* uses scenes with Q as a way to invoke moments from the previous films. The 2012 film again reuses the famous "joking" line with the introduction of Ben Whishaw as Q.

> [sitting next to each other in the National Gallery]
>
> Q: I'm your new quartermaster.
>
> Bond: You must be joking.
>
> Q: Why? Because I'm not wearing a lab coat?
>
> Bond: Because you still have spots.
>
> Q: My complexion is hardly relevant.

Bond: Your competence is.

Q: Age is no guarantee of efficiency.

Bond: And youth is no guarantee of innovation.

Q: Well, I'll hazard I can do more damage on my laptop sitting in my pajamas before my first cup of Earl Grey than you can do in a year in the field.

Bond: Oh, so why do you need me?

Q: Every now and then, a trigger has to be pulled.

Bond: Or not pulled. It's hard to know which in your pajamas.

Later in the conversation, Q gives Bond a new gun and a radio that can be used as a distress signal. Still, 007 acts disappointed.

Bond: A gun and a radio. Not exactly Christmas, is it?

Q: Were you expecting an exploding pen? We don't really go in for that anymore.[101]

Of course, every huge 007 fan knows the exploding pen is a reference to *Goldeneye*, where Bond uses the gadget to defeat former 006.

Skyfall also pays tribute to *Goldfinger* late in the film. Bond must get M out of the city and needs a new vehicle, so he stops by the old MI6 garage to pick up the 1964 Aston Martin he drove

---

[101] *Skyfall*. 2012.

in *Goldfinger*. As the two drive away, the solo guitar part of the Bond theme plays in the background.

The film also references the car's famous ejector seat.

M: [as they begin to drive] Not very comfortable is it?

Bond: [puts his finger over the red ejector seat button] You going to complain the whole way?

M: Oh, go on then, eject me. See if I care.[102]

Although it's much more subtle, the 50-year-old scotch that Silva offers to Bond when they first meet is also a slight reference to the series, as the film's release marked the 50th anniversary of the Bond series.

These nostalgic moments work excellently when juxtaposed with the film's ultimate meaning.

Skyfall depicts the MI6 at a crossroads. The beginning of the film shows Bond's death, and the bureaucrats are pushing M into retirement. The golden age of espionage is dead.

Sometimes, the film expresses this meaning delicately, like with the beginning of Q and 007's conversation at the National Gallery in London.

Bond is looking at the 19th century painting called "The Fighting Temeraire," painted by the famous British artist J.M.W. Turner. Done in 1838, it showcases a battleship getting tugged to her last berth.

---

[102] *Skyfall*. 2012.

Q: [looking at the painting] Always makes me feel a little melancholy. Grand, old warship being ignominiously hauled away for scrap. [to Bond] The inevitability of time, don't you think? What do you see?

Bond: A bloody, big ship.[103]

Another delicate hint to this theme is in the Adele "Skyfall" song lyrics, which come immediately after Bond's supposed death.

This is the end
Hold your breath and count to ten
Feel the earth move and then
Hear my heart burst again
For this is the end[104]

In other cases, the film's meaning is quite clear. At a hearing with the British Parliament, M receives an extended lecture from parliament member Clair Dowar.

Dowar: It's as if you insist on pretending we still live in a golden age of espionage, where human intelligence was the only resource available. Well I find this rather old-fashioned belief demonstrates a reckless disregard... [a fellow parliament member interrupts her].[105]

During Dowar's rant, M is the old battleship getting tugged to the shipyard to be scrapped, but the Turner painting can also

---

[103] *Skyfall*. 2012.
[104] Adele. "Skyfall." XL Recordings. XLS593CD, 2012, compact disc.
[105] *Skyfall*. 2012.

be seen as a metaphor for 007 and the MI6. Bond's way of doing things isn't the best anymore.

But that's not always true. When Moneypenny greets Bond in Macau, she seems a bit surprised to see he uses a straight razor, but after Bond says he likes to do some things the old-fashioned way, she says "Sometimes the old ways are the best."

The Skyfall lodge gamekeeper, Kincade (Albert Finney), repeats the same line when all he and Bond have to fend off Silva and his men are a couple of hunting rifles, a few knives and a couple sticks of dynamite, "sometimes the old ways are the best."

With this, the film seems to be pushing back on the idea that old is synonymous with outdated. Bond and Q help lay out the subtle differences when together they claim "age is no guarantee of efficiency" but "youth is no guarantee of innovation."

M's counterargument to the British Parliament works as the film's final claim that there's still a use for old-fashioned ways.

> M: Chairman, Ministers, today, I've repeatedly heard how irrelevant my department has become. "Why do we need agents, the double-0 section? Isn't it all rather quaint?" Well, I suppose I see a different world than you do and the truth is that what I see frightens me. I'm frightened because our enemies are no longer known to us. They do not exist on a map. They're not nations, they're individuals. And look around you. Who do you fear? Can you see a face, a uniform, a flag? No. Our world is not more transparent now; it's more opaque. It's in the shadows. That's where we

must do battle. So before you declare us irrelevant, ask yourselves, how safe do you feel? Just one more thing to say, my late husband was a great lover of poetry, and, um, I suppose some of it sunk in, despite my best intentions. And here today, I remember this, I think from Tennyson: "We are not now that strength which in old days moved earth and heaven, that which we are, we are. One equal temper of heroic hearts, made weak by time and fate, but strong in will. To strive, to seek, to find, and *not* to yield."[106]

As she finishes her poem, Silva bursts in and begins murdering civilians and security guards at the hearing. He nearly gets to M, but then Bond, the supposedly outdated spy, saves her and the entire British Parliament, with the help of Moneypenny and Gareth Mallory (the Chairman of the Intelligence and Security Committee).

At the beginning of the film, Mallory breaks the forced retirement news to M, telling her she "had a great run," but his reaction to take up arms and shoot back at Silva acts as his way of converting his allegiance to the MI6. After M's death, Mallory assumes the title and becomes the new leader of the MI6.

As the new M in *Spectre*, Mallory continues this fight against the head of the Joint Security Service, who is named C. The Spectre crime organization has partnered with C in order to gain access to an unlimited amount of intelligence cameras from around the world.

---

[106] *Skyfall*. 2012.

To C in the film, M again makes his case for the existence of the MI6.

> C: The double-0 program is prehistoric. Come on, M, you can't really tell me that one man in the field can compete with all of this (his highly sophisticated surveillance system) running around out there with his license to kill.
>
> M: Have you ever had to kill a man, Max (C's real name)? Have you? To pull that trigger, you have to be sure. Yes, you investigate, analyze, assess, target and then you have to look him in the eye, and you make the call. And all the drones, bugs, cameras, transcripts, all the surveillance in the world can't tell you what to do next. A license to kill is also a license NOT to kill.[107]

Bond proves this to be true; rather than shooting an unarmed Blofeld on Westminster Bridge at the end of *Spectre*, he stands down and allows M to take him into custody.

While the characters in both films fight for their method of saving the world, all of these scenes are also the films' way of arguing for the continued existence of the Bond series. At its core, *Skyfall* is suggesting "the old ways" in which the series made its films are outdated. The series can't continue to exploit women and contain other outdated practices if it wishes to remain contemporary.

But at the same time, nothing beats that Aston Martin car from 1964. And the new films aren't going to have exploding pens, but boy, wasn't that a great gadget in *Goldeneye*?

---

[107] *Spectre*. 2015.

It doesn't get much more self-aware than that.

Spectre continues this idea with a counterargument to the digital age. By all means, humankind should embrace technology, but there still isn't a substitute for human interaction. Even Blofeld helps make this point prior to torturing Bond.

> Blofeld: As you know all too well, dear Madeleine, a man lives inside his head. That's where the seed of his soul is. James and I were both present recently when a man was deprived of his eyes and the most astonishing thing happened, [to Bond] didn't you notice? He wasn't there anymore. He had gone even though he was still alive, so this brief moment between life and death, there was nobody inside his skull. Most odd.[108]

While the monologue works as a way for Blofeld to appear more villainous, he's actually pointing out what makes human life different. A drone will never have a soul, and it can't look someone in the eye to ultimately decide whether or not to pull the trigger.

Bond's way of doing things isn't dead, and he doesn't need to retire. He's not a washed up, old warship that needs to be taken to the scrap yard for parts. And neither is the series.

The old films are flawed but largely still enjoyable. As the poem that M quotes states, the series will continue "to strive, to seek, to find, and *not* to yield" as it continues to modernize in the 21st century.

---

[108] *Spectre.* 2015.

9

"NOBODY DOES IT BETTER"

Music is an essential part of the human experience. Our radio alarm clock or phone jingle wakes us and gets us out of bed every morning. Then, we play music in the shower, on the commute to and from work, and sometimes in the office. It's hard to even get in an elevator without hearing some kind of tune.

Today, it's easier to access music than ever before in history. With Pandora, Spotify, YouTube and others, we have access to giant libraries available on various devices and the most extreme niche radio channels on Sirius XM. Don't forget the good, old-fashioned car radio.

Music is so ingrained in human life that it's easy to take it for granted. Music in the Bond film series isn't any different. It's become such a part of the series over the years that it can sometimes go unnoticed and unappreciated, but in actuality, the music may be the best way in which the series stays current with its audience.

Stop and think about it -- there are very few action films or series that don't have a great theme song. *Star Wars, Indiana*

Jones, Mission Impossible, Lord of the Rings and *Superman* are some of the most popular action film series of all time, and they all have fantastic theme songs. Even people who haven't seen those films could probably listen to their theme songs and know their origin.

To a lesser extent, theme songs from *Jurassic Park, The Terminator, The Godfather and Harry Potter* (if one considers the last two part of the action genre) are widely recognizable as well.

The Bond theme song isn't any different. Fans would be able to identify the unique guitar riff, composed by Monty Norman and arranged by John Barry, anywhere. The "dum di-di-di-di dum dum dum" sound is so simple and yet so riveting and suave, especially with the solo guitar combined with the brass instrumental.

The Bond theme should probably be at the top of most lists, but such rankings would be very subjective, and there are so many great action film theme songs. However, it's hard to argue there's a theme song that epitomizes a single character better than Bond's.

It's as if the solo guitar in the music is a representation of 007 himself, going about his business -- killing and sleeping with whomever -- to accomplish his mission. In the middle of the theme, the brass instruments break out, perhaps personifying the chaos that often surrounds him, and yet, eventually, it's back to the solo guitar, indicating that no matter what, Bond is going to remain a calm, steady presence.

007 is the definition of cool, and so is his theme song.

The Bond theme didn't really begin as a series theme song, but as the instrumental theme for the main titles in *Dr. No*. Then starting with *From Russia with Love*, each subsequent film would have its own title theme that played during the opening credits.

Eventually, this became as big a part of the 007 series tradition as the Bond girls, vodka martinis "shaken, not stirred" and his Walther PPK. The individual theme songs were unique, giving each film something else the audience could use to identify them.

For example, "You Only Live Twice" has a slight nod to Japan with its inclusion of traditional Asian musical riffs. The "On Your Majesty's Secret Service" title theme offered simplicity, as the only theme (other than the Bond main theme song) not to include lyrics. It's straightforwardness directly ties with the goal of the film to return to the Bond roots following an over-the-top plot line in *You Only Live Twice*.

There may be a few occasions throughout the series where the film wasn't all that enjoyable, but at least the title music was. This allows audience members to find some redeeming quality in even the poorly written or directed Bond films.

It's also not as if little-known artists were singing these title themes. The series orchestrated to have famous and popular artists perform these songs.

Matt Monro performed "From Russia with Love," which was arranged by Barry, for the second film. Only the instrumental version of the song plays during the opening credits, but the song with Monro's voice is part of the film's ending. Starting with *Goldfinger*, the title themes would feature world-renowned artists during the opening credits.

The series couldn't have picked a better first featured artist than Shirley Bassey.

By 1964, the Welsh singer had released four albums that peaked in the Top 15 in the UK and had several singles reach the Top 5. She made her American television debut in November 1960, appearing on *The Ed Sullivan Show*.[109]

She wasn't as popular in the United States, but even American audiences loved her song, "Goldfinger," where she uses her signature powerful voice. The single peaked in the U.S. at No. 8 while the soundtrack to the film hit No. 1 in 1965.[110]

The series would use Bassey two more times to sing title themes "Diamonds are Forever" and "Moonraker" during the 1970's. Her three title theme appearances in the series are still the most for any artist, and while she continues to be a bigger icon in Europe than the United States, Bassey set the standard for title themes in the series.

Thunderball doesn't have as notable of a theme song, but music plays as intricate a role in the film as any in the series.

Based on my own calculations, more than 24 minutes, or roughly 19 percent, of *Thunderball* takes place under water. A vast majority of those underwater scenes are featured in the final 90 minutes, meaning about a quarter of the film's last hour

[109] Williams, John L. (2010). *Miss Shirley Bassey*. London: Quercus. pp. 219. ISBN 978-1-84724-974-6.
[110] "Shirley Bassey Chart History," *Billboard*, https://www.billboard.com/music/shirley-bassey.

and a half is under water. That length of time with no dialogue was astonishing for a 1960's film. By today's standards, *Thunderball* probably wouldn't work because according to a Microsoft study, the attention span of the average person in the 21st century is shorter than it was 50 years ago.[111]

It's unlikely a film could be made again with such long sequences under water. That's probably at least one of the reasons why Jack Schwartzman undertook remaking the movie with virtually no underwater sequences in the mid-1980's, renaming it *Never Say Never Again*. It's the only theatrical release of a Bond film not canon with the rest of the series, and it's the only official remake.

While some have criticized the original *Thunderball* for a slow pace due to all the underwater scenes, the action sequences and underwater cinematography also helped make it unique and one of the best Bond films ever. Playing a large part in that was the music.

Without dialogue, the film keeps its viewers interested with a captivating musical score. Instruments don't work under water, but sometimes, it feels as though the music has a hollow sound to it, almost as if their music is coming from the bathtub or another aquatic area. This further helps place the audience in the tropical scene with Bond and the other characters.

The film's theme title song works in the same fashion. The brass section simultaneously blaring its musical notes while bubbles fill the screen gives the audience the illusion of being under

---

[111] Kevin McSpadden. "You Now Have a Shorter Attention Span Than a Goldfish," *Time*, May 14, 2015, http://time.com/3858309/attention-spans-goldfish/.

water. The series repeats this trick a few more times in theme songs for *The Spy Who Loved Me* and *For Your Eyes Only*, but it definitely worked best with "Thunderball."

The title theme for *Moonraker* again conveys a general aspect of the film, but rather than water, it's a "spacey" aura -- lots of high notes played at a deliberate pace to express how most believe being in outer space would feel.

However, action films in the 1960's that featured a lot of dialogue also needed great music to succeed. Without the technology to showcase many action sequences, music was the best way in which a filmmaker conveyed action and drama until the late 1970's.

No scene in the series expresses this idea better than when a tarantula crawls into bed with Bond during *Dr. No*. For today's audience, the background music in this scene is highly dramatized, but the film couldn't have asked for a better score. The music expresses a "creepy-crawly" type feel as the spider moves up Bond's arm, and then the horn section blasts its notes concurrently with 007 smashing the tarantula to death with his shoe.

To anyone watching this scene for the first time in the modern era, it's laughable. But that's how action films were made at the time. Music played a large part in making this scene memorable, and so many other early scenes of 007. Without them, who knows if the series would have become as popular as it did.

Tom Jones, who sings the title song "Thunderball", wasn't as famous as Bassey, but he became extremely popular upon the song's release. In the same year, Jones also sang the theme song to *What's New Pussycat?*, and both theme songs helped him win the Grammy Award for Best New Artist in 1966.[112]

The series had another up-and-coming starlet sing the next title theme "You Only Live Twice" with Nancy Sinatra. She was just beginning her career, but her last name obviously gave her merit to be the next great voice of the series' ever-growing popular title theme songs.

It's definitely worth asking whether the film series helped shape Bassey, Jones and Sinatra into bigger stars or if their stardom helped make the Bond title theme songs a longstanding series tradition. The simple answer is it was probably a little bit of both, but after Bassey's second title song in 1971, the series was eyeing one of the biggest artists in England's history -- Paul McCartney.

"Live and Let Die", performed by McCartney and Wings, is arguably the greatest of all the 007 title theme songs. Even more importantly, though, it's just a fantastic rock song and, culturally, it placed the Bond title theme songs on another level.

McCartney's "Live and Let Die" is one of his most famous songs. He still plays it at concerts. If he left it off his setlist, his crowd would walk away just as disappointed as if he hadn't played "Hey Jude", "Let it Be", or "Maybe I'm Amazed."

It's hard to believe one of the most famous songs McCartney ever wrote was a theme song to a movie. After all, he was a

---

[112] "Grammy Awards 1966," *Awards & Shows,*
http://www.awardsandshows.com/features/grammy-awards-1966-241.html.

founding member of perhaps the greatest rock and roll band of all time.

McCartney's "Live and Let Die" transcends the film. It's probably more likely that a 20-year-old recognizes the song's famous and incredible *bum bum bum, bum bum bum, bum bum* riff than be able to name what Bond film it's from originally.

McCartney continuing to play "Live and Let Die" at concerts supports another important idea -- once you perform a Bond title theme song, you are always part of the series' long history. Again, these songs are one of the greatest 007 traditions, and viewers are enthralled with who will sing each new entry as much as they are with who will play the next Bond girl or, after a certain amount of time, the next 007.

For his efforts, McCartney and his wife, Linda, were nominated for the Best Original Song Academy Award in 1973. They didn't win, losing to "The Way We Were" from the film of the same title, but it wouldn't be the last Academy Award nomination for the series in the Best Original Song category.[113]

Including "Live and Let Die," five title theme songs have been nominated in the Best Original Song category at the Academy Awards. In the same era of McCartney, Carly Simon's "Nobody Does It Better" and Sheena Easton's "For Your Eyes Only" received nominations in 1977 and 1981, respectively.[114]

---

[113] "James Bond at the Oscars," *James Bond Museum*, April 13, 2019, http://www.007museum.com/oscar007.htm.
[114] "James Bond at the Oscars," http://www.007museum.com/oscar007.htm.

Like McCartney, Simon performing the title theme for *The Spy Who Loved Me* is another example of the Bond series landing a famous contemporary artist for its longstanding opening credits tradition. Simon didn't win the Oscar, but she would about a decade later for a different opening title song "Let the River Run," for *Working Girl* (1988).[115]

Easton's "For Your Eyes Only" didn't get her the Oscar either, but it remains one of the best title themes in the series and followed in the footsteps of *Thunderball* by using "aquatic sounding" musical notes. There aren't as many as there were in *Thunderball*, but *For Your Eyes Only* does feature a few different underwater scenes.

After Easton's beautiful theme, the Bond series would have to wait 31 years before receiving another nomination in the Best Original Song category at the Academy Awards. This time, though, the series took home the hardware.

In 2012, Adele's "Skyfall" for the film of the same title won the award. The song also won Best Original Song at the Golden Globes and the Grammys, as well as the Brit Award for British Single of the Year.[116]

"Skyfall" was a success among fans too. It climbed to No. 2 on the UK Singles Chart, which tied Duran Duran's "A View to a

---

[115] "James Bond at the Oscars,"
http://www.007museum.com/oscar007.htm.
[116] "Skyfall Awards," *IMDB*, April 13, 2019,
https://www.imdb.com/title/tt1074638/awards.

Kill" as the highest-charted Bond title theme on the UK Singles Chart.[117]

However, that record didn't stand very long. Sam Smith's "Writing's on the Wall" reached all the way to No. 1 on the UK Singles Chart list in 2015 when it opened for *Spectre*. The tune also won Best Original Song at the Golden Globes and Academy Awards.[118]

The selection of Adele and Smith as the two latest artists to construct Bond title theme songs cements the idea that the series uses music as a way to stay current and modern. In 2012, the series could have very easily used a classic rock band or a popular artist from the 1970's or 1980's, and it wouldn't have felt at all out of place. If anything, it would have fit better with the stereotypical Bond viewer, who lived through the Cold War.

But that's never been what the theme songs have been about in the series. The title themes have usually featured one of the hottest, most popular artists of that time, helping to keep the series appealing to a young audience. Even Adele fans who may have never seen a Bond film wanted to at least tune in to the buzz around the release of *Skyfall*, so they could hear the latest happenings about Adele.

Just before Adele's "Skyfall," Alicia Keys and Jack White of The White Stripes teamed up to perform "Another Way to Die" for *Quantum of Solace*. The song didn't reach the same notoriety as

---

[117] Rob Copsey, "Every James Bond theme ever and where they charted," *Official Charts*, September 8, 2015, https://www.officialcharts.com/chart-news/every-james-bond-theme-ever-and-where-they-charted__10670/.
[118] "Writing's On The Wall," *Song Facts*, April 13, 2019, https://www.songfacts.com/facts/sam-smith/writings-on-the-wall.

its successors, but it's another example where the series used popular musicians.

Whether the title theme artist was just up and coming or well established, a contemporary sound has always been the most important aspect.

Perhaps an even better example of this idea is Duran Duran, who performed "A View to a Kill" in 1985. The tune's synthpop is reminiscent of *The Terminator* (1984) theme, helping to make it the quintessential mid-1980's rock song.

It didn't win any awards or receive any nominations, but as previously mentioned, it became the first Bond theme song to hit No. 2 on the UK Singles Chart, and it would remain the only one for 27 years. "A View to a Kill" also reached No. 1 on the U.S. Billboard Hot 100.[119]

In many ways, Duran Duran's theme song is the biggest redeeming quality of the otherwise mundane final Roger Moore Bond film that is *A View to a Kill*.

Seven Bond theme songs have reached the Top 10 on the U.S. Billboard Hot 100, but "A View to a Kill" is the only one to climb all the way to No. 1. "Live and Let Die" and "Nobody Does it Better" fell just short of the top spot at No. 2, and "For Your Eyes Only" reached the Top 5, peaking at No. 4.[120]

---

[119] "Writing's On The Wall," https://www.songfacts.com/facts/sam-smith/writings-on-the-wall.
[120] Joe Lynch, "007 on Hot 100: See James Bond Songs From Lowest to Highest Charting," *Billboard*, July 25, 2017, https://www.billboard.com/articles/news/6753813/james-bond-songs-hot-100-highest-charting.

"Goldfinger," "Skyfall" and Madonna's "Die Another Day" all made it to No. 8 on the U.S. Billboard Hot 100.[121] Madonna's title theme in 2002 is yet another example of a well-established star singing a Bond song.

While her career did peak more than a decade prior to the film's release, it doesn't get much bigger than an artist who only needs one name.

Seven years prior to Madonna's "Die Another Day, the series used Tina Turner to sing "Goldeneye." Turner is another example of an artist signing a title theme more than 20 years after her career began. But Turner was still extremely popular in the mid-1990's; her album titled "What's Love Got to Do with It" hit No. 1 in the UK during 1993.[122]

After Turner, the series returned to using new starlet artists with Sheryl Crow for "Tomorrow Never Dies" in 1997. At the time of the film's release, Crow had only produced two albums,[123] but she would become very popular in the early 2000's after her induction into Bond theme song history.

Following "A View to a Kill," the series employed A-ha to sing "The Living Daylights." A-ha has sold 100 million records worldwide,[124] so they are hardly a one-hit wonder, but they are

---

[121] Lynch, "007 on Hot 100: See James Bond Songs From Lowest to Highest Charting," https://www.billboard.com/articles/news/6753813/james-bond-songs-hot-100-highest-charting.
[122]
https://www.officialcharts.com/search/albums/what's%20love%20got%20to%20do%20with%20it/.
[123] "Sheryl Crow Discography," *All Music*, April 13, 2019, https://www.allmusic.com/artist/sheryl-crow-mn0000080780/discography.
[124] "a-ha," *Music Norway*, April 13, 2019, *https://musicnorway.no/artist/a-ha-2/*.

an even bigger generational band than Duran Duran. You'll be hard pressed to find someone who can name an A-ha song other than their biggest hit, "Take on Me."

But even though they didn't transcend the series like some of the other theme songs, win any awards or climb the U.S. Billboard Hot 100, the A-ha theme song still achieved its goal. The use of contemporary artists in the Bond title theme songs is perhaps the best way the series continues to remain relevant and connected with the youth of western society.

Without the enduring title theme songs, the Bond series wouldn't have made nearly the same cultural impact it did in the second half of the 20th century and continues to do in the new millennium.

10

FROM THE WALTHER PPK TO THE INVISIBLE CAR

In the early 20th century, the Spanish-American philosopher George Santayana famously coined the phrase "those who cannot remember the past are condemned to repeat it."[125] When it comes to James Bond, though, fans remember just about everything, and history still seems to repeat itself.

As much as the series has evolved over the years, it seems to do so in a circular motion, returning to its roots every so often. It's reminiscent of another historical theory.

---

[125] Matthew Caleb Flamm, "George Santaya," Internet Encyclopedia of Philosophy, April 13, 2019, https://www.iep.utm.edu/santayan/.

Figure 2: The History Gyre

Northern Highlands Regional High School in Bergen County, New Jersey is probably most famous for producing former FBI director James Comey, but English teachers in the high school lecture what they call the History Gyre.[126] The theory specifically states that history not only repeats itself, but

---

[126] Dr. Thomas Rooney, *English teacher and Department Chair,* Needham High School in Needham, MA.

civilization moves in an evolutionary circle between four different stages: primitive, hierarchical, classical and decadent.

As the illustration showcases, the primitive stage features revolutionary ideals and a shared belief in new order while the final stage – decadent – emphasizes spectacle and excess. In between, religion, written law and superstition reign supreme in the hierarchic stage, and in the third stage – classical – society is at its very best self, reaching its peak.

At its core, the theory is rather simplistic. Civilization at most points in history cannot be classified completely into one stage, but it's an interesting theory that nonetheless can also be applied to the circular evolution of the Bond series. In particular, the primitive and decadent stages apply to 007.

Through Bond history, each film finds a way to top the previous one. Whether through action sequences, plot twists, gadgets, or something else, the next Bond film is always the biggest and boldest. Well, that is, until the action is so unrealistic and over the top, that the series has no choice but to return to the beginning -- the primitive stage.

Compared to the other films in the series, *Dr. No* is rather primitive. Its plot is somewhat complex, especially for the early 1960's, but the action sequences are straightforward, and Bond's only gadget is his newly acquired Walther PPK. Q doesn't make his first appearance in the series until the next film.

In that next film, *From Russia with Love*, Bond has a secret compartment in his new suitcase, which also explodes tear gas if not opened properly. Rosa Klebb (Lotte Lenya), one of the primary villains in the film, has a poisonous knife pop out of the tip of her shoe. With this, the series has left the primitive stage.

Goldfinger and *Thunderball* are the Bond film equivalents of the classical stage. For one, the movies are generally regarded as the two best with Connery, and two of the better films in the entire series. Bond's Aston Martin car with the ejector seat, 007 strapped to Goldfinger's chair with a laser approaching his body, Bond's jetpack and Largo's shark tank are just some of the classic moments those two films produced. These gadgets and plot points aren't very realistic but at least believable to a certain extent.

But to top this, in *You Only Live Twice*, Bond undergoes a ridiculous "face transformation" that's supposed to make him Japanese and nearly goes into outer space. The whole concept of the crime organization of Spectre capturing spaceships in outer space is absurd, along with Bond's ridiculously looking single-seated helicopter (autogyro). There's little chance that thing could fly let alone single-handedly beat a squad of war helicopters.

Despite the popularity of *You Only Live Twice*, the series producers were apparently aware they couldn't progress along this path much longer because the films would continue to get more preposterous and silly.

Therefore, the series returned to the beginning -- the primitive stage -- in *On Her Majesty's Secret Service*. George Lazenby's only adventure as Bond was the grittiest entry of the decade. Not only does 007 fall in love and suffer heartbreak, but he has very few gadgets to help him against Blofeld.

The *coolest* thing Bond does in the film is probably his chest-down slide along the ice while shooting a machine gun toward Blofeld's lair. That's a far cry from a single-seated helicopter.

As previously stated, even the *On Her Majesty's Secret Service* title theme provides a simplistic, primitive feeling, as it's the only theme song without lyrics other than the original Bond theme song, which is now considered more of a "series theme" than the title theme of *Dr. No*.

But the series didn't stay this primitive. It branched out again with the moon buggy chase scene in *Diamonds are Forever*, and the crocodile trap in *Live and Let Die*. Each border on the line of absurd, but more than anything, each scene is fun. By the time *The Man with the Golden Gun* comes out, the series is completely immersed in Roger Moore's cheesy and somewhat over-the-top humor. In that film, Bond pulls off an Evil Knievel-type jump and wears a third nipple as a disguise.

With *The Spy Who Loved Me*, the series has returned to its classical period. The film is essentially *You Only Live Twice* but in ocean form, as the villain captures both Russian and American nuclear ships and then uses the weapons to begin nuclear war. But with the perfect combination of violence, humor and gadgets, it's Moore's best entry in the series.

The film also provides the audience another shark tank, one of the series' best Bond girls (Barbara Bach as Anya Amasova), and one of the most memorable villains in Jaws (Richard Kiel).

At the end of every 007 film, the final credits say "Bond will return in" whatever the title is for the following movie. In *The Spy Who Loved Me* credits, that next film is *For Your Eyes Only*, but after the financial success of *Star Wars*, the Bond series called an audible and tried to ride the success wave of perhaps the greatest Sci-Fi film ever made.

From a box office standpoint, *Moonraker* was a hit, but it's one of the worst films of the series. It starts out fine, but then goes quickly downhill when Bond heads into outer space to a secret space station that looks to be bigger than Hawaii. How the Americans and Russians didn't know it was there is anybody's guess.

It didn't help that the film's special effects were dated upon release. Watching it today, it looks even older than it is, especially when comparing it to the *Star Wars* series.

After the release of *Moonraker*, the series had nowhere to go -- except back to the beginning. So again, the series went for a reset, even with the same actor playing Bond, in *For Your Eyes Only*.

The first 007 film of the 1980's featured very few gadgets and a simple Cold-War plot that has the British and Russians chasing down the ATAC system, which is a device used by the British to communicate and coordinate their fleet. It's a grittier, edgier entry that doesn't feature a giant explosion or army attack in the climactic scene.

That's probably why it isn't as well known to the casual Bond fan, but diehard fans of the series know it to be one of Moore's best films and perhaps the most underrated film in the series.

Similar to the last 1960's series reset, the 007 films didn't stay primitive very long. The final two Moore entries, *Octopussy* and *A View to a Kill*, are largely considered average at best and don't have any classic scenes or moments. That problem continued in the late 1980's with Timothy Dalton's version of Bond in *The Living Daylights* and *License to Kill*.

A lot of fans like to blame Dalton, calling him the worst Bond, for nearly killing the series at the end of the 1980's. The closest the series came to a hit may have been in 1987. Apparently, there's a small sector of fans who loved *The Living Daylights*.

Consider Jalopink staff writer Justin T. Westbrook one of them:

"You know that '80s Bond movie where the Aston Martin has skis, the Bond girl plays the cello, and the Taliban are good guys? I love that one! What was it called? *The Living Daylights!*"[127]

How the series was portraying race and women, especially with the emergence of AIDS, was all coming to the forefront at the same time. As previously discussed, the series' Bond girl character took a giant nosedive during this era too.

But the biggest problem was in the plots and stories. None of these films had great writing, and it led to the longest gap (six years) between films in the series' history.

With the release of *Goldeneye*, the series was firmly back on course. One could argue the film returned to the series' roots, but really, it was a return to Bond's classical roots -- a vengeful villain out to send England back to the stone age. The film uses just the right amount of gadgets and humor while giving the

---

[127] Justin T. Westbrook, "*The Living Daylights*: The Good Bond Movie You Can Never Remember The Name Of," Jalopnik, August 27, 2015, https://jalopnik.com/the-living-daylights-the-good-bond-movie-you-can-never-1726850812.

audience a slightly over-the-top but very well-done and memorable tank chase scene through St. Petersburg.

The opening scene of *Goldeneye* alone eliminates the possibility of the film being in the primitive stage. 007 tries to fly away from the Russian base he has rigged to explode, but he rolls out of the cockpit door while fighting a Russian soldier. Bond defeats the soldier and grabs a motorcycle to chase down the plane, which is slowly moving towards the end of the runway. But before he gets to the plane, both it and Bond on the motorcycle fall off a giant cliff.

No need to worry, though, because in midair, Bond flies down fast enough to catch up to the plane, pulls himself into the cockpit and takes control of the plane before it crashes -- all to the backdrop of the exploding Russian base.

It was absolutely cool, especially on the big screen. After a six-year absence, this was the series' big way of saying -- Bond was back and better than ever. But by no means was *Goldeneye* going to be a barebones spy film.

Brosnan's Bond used a lot of gadgets during his four films, but none bigger than the invisible car in *Die Another Day*. Again, this took the series into the decadent stage.

While the opening scene of *Goldeneye* was decadent, neighboring on absurd, audiences seemed to accept it. But there's no realism in an invisible car. Anyone over the age of 13 considered the insertion of Q's latest update to the Aston Martin nonsensical.

That wasn't the only aspect of *Die Another Day* that had no hope of realism. The primary villain of the film, Colonel Tan-Sun

Moon, undergoes a genetic procedure that turns him into the white Gustav Graves. Scientists are nowhere close to discovering how to change the race of a human being.

On top of that, Graves owns a hotel made entirely of ice. That was the cherry on top of perhaps the most unrealistic film of the series.

Not that *Die Another Day* was a bad film. The way the story unfolds is eerily similar to *Goldfinger*. It's just not realistic, and there was no way to top its absurdity. How do you beat an invisible car?

The series was probably due for a reset anyway, but 007 returned to the primitive stage again with Daniel Craig's debut in *Casino Royale*. The film showcased no gadgets -- it's one of the few films that Q doesn't even make an appearance -- and it makes Bond's transformation into 007 the focal point of the story. That and his complicated relationship with Vesper Lynd.

Craig's four films as Bond are certainly different. As previously argued, there's a concerted effort to be far more accepting of all denominations -- including races, genders and sexual preferences. But that hasn't stopped the 007 evolutionary circle.

While the series hasn't seen a truly decadent film under Craig, it's headed in that direction. Craig's most recent Bond film, *Spectre*, featured him hanging outside a flying helicopter while engaged in a fistfight. He also easily survives a plane crash where the plane loses its tail and wings.

Similar to Jaws or Oddjob, *Spectre* featured a giant henchman called Hinx. There's much more realism to Hinx than any of the previously villainous henchmen, but what he can do still borders on the absurd.

Just like the Bond codename theory, the series producers aren't conscious of this evolutionary circle -- it's happened naturally over the decades. But it's an important concept because it's one of the better ways in which the series reflects the ebbs and flows of modern civilization.

Taking a broad look at the human history, one could suggest the History Gyre moves very slowly through the four stages. An argument can be made that the last instance civilization returned to primitive was the fall of the Roman Empire, where "barbaric" tribes ruled and knowledge of written history was lost, leading to the Dark Ages.

Maybe that means the next return to the primitive stage will come in the form of a zombie apocalypse, which is so often portrayed in today's film and television. Or perhaps a real life Bond villain will actually reset civilization with nuclear war.

However, it doesn't have to take such drastic historical moments to complete the History Gyre. For example, Donald Trump becoming president of the United States could be viewed as a move back to the primitive stage. Trump campaigned on the notion that he would "Make America Great Again" -- a slogan that helped start a revolution among working-class Americans.

His supporters have often been quoted saying they voted for Trump to "drain the swamp," which could be viewed as a "rejection" of the established early 21st century American empire. Both revolution and rejection of empire are key components to the primitive stage.

With this in mind, the 13 American colonies declaring independence from Great Britain in 1776 could also be viewed as a return to the primitive stage.

But again, it's just about impossible to classify any one period of time into one stage. The 2016 U.S. election results could also signify a return to the decadent stage, where propaganda, militarism and dictatorship rule the world.

The Bond films work the same way, as each film can feature multiple elements from the different stages.

In summary, on a large scale including all of human history, one might be able to try and fit the entire existence of the United States into one stage. But with a much more refined lens, America has repeated the History Gyre several times over since Bond's debut in 1962.

That helps explain why the series moves between the stages so quickly. Because as much as Bond has influenced western culture, society also has an impact on the 007 series.

One of the best examples of this is the aforementioned inclusion of *Moonraker* following the explosion of *Star Wars*. While *Moonraker* was one of Ian Fleming's novels, the series changed the plot drastically, turning it into a Sci-Fi film.

The same could be said for the Jaws character, who appears in *The Spy Who Loved Me* and *Moonraker*. Jaws is based on a henchman from Fleming's novel, but the name "Jaws" is clearly a reference to the blockbuster film that hit theaters two years before *The Spy Who Loved Me*.

But, the series hasn't always adopted what is popular at the time. While in bed with Jill Masterson in *Goldfinger*, Bond reaches down for more champagne when he realizes it's "lost its chill." When Masterson questions 007 for getting up and insisting he needs cold champagne, he says:

> Bond: My dear girl, there are some things that just aren't done, such as drinking Dom Perignon '53 above the temperature of 38 degrees Fahrenheit. That's as bad as listening to the Beatles without earmuffs.[128]

I'm no champagne expert, but a quick google search actually indicates the perfect temperature for Dom Perignon is about 45 degrees, so Bond's math is a little bit off.[129] More importantly, the series threw in this obvious Beatles diss, which is rather comical 55 years later.

At the time, though, it was appropriate. Remember, *Goldfinger* came out in 1964 when the Beatles were front and center of the British Invasion. In those early days of the band, their fan base was more screaming teenage girls than anything. The 007 series had (and still somewhat has) the opposite audience -- 13 to 45-year-old males.

Bond is speaking to his fans when he makes the joke about the Beatles. The modern equivalent would be Craig's Bond saying he would rather go deaf than listen to the Jonas Brothers.

---

[128] *Goldfinger*. 1964.
[129] Cynthia Measom, "How To Serve Dom Perignon," *Leaf*, April 18, 2019, https://www.leaf.tv/articles/how-to-serve-dom-perignon/.

There's likely very little audience overlap between the 007 series and that band. If the Jonas Brothers end up becoming one of the most influential rock and roll bands of all time, audiences would laugh at that joke in 2074 too.

But for the most part, the series keeps adapting to what's popular in an attempt to appeal to modern audiences. With Craig as Bond, the series' producers and writers have showcased a grittier 007 -- one more likely to fall into the primitive stage.

Again, realism grew into an important part of the action genre. As previously mentioned, *Batman Begins* was heavily influential in this change. The new Batman trilogy director, Christopher Nolan, told *Screen Rant* in 2018 that each of his three Batman films belong in different genres, classifying them into these genres: "a heroes journey," crime, and war.[130]

Simply put, they're superhero films, but it would be ignorant to ignore their influence on the action genre. The straightforward, good versus evil, blockbuster action film died about 15 years ago, and with its death came the rise of the anti-hero. This obviously impacted where the 007 series was going with Craig.

The series couldn't keep making its films with the same slapstick style of the 1970's and 1980's. Even Brosnan's puns became out of date. The series had to adapt in the 21st century, and as it always has, it did.

---

[130] Timothy Lammers, "Christopher Nolan Says His Batman Films Are Each a Different Genre," *Screen Rant*, May 12, 2018, https://screenrant.com/christopher-nolan-batman-films-genre/.

It evolved back to the primitive stage, stripping the series of its silliness and making Bond more real with a new sense of vulnerability. Whether the series completes another circle is to be determined. It may stay primarily in the primitive stage for awhile until there's another major change in the action genre.

In some ways, it's a fitting switch. After all, an anti-hero is someone who performs immoral deeds and sometimes acts primarily out of self-interest but usually with the best intentions.

Sounds like Bond may have been an anti-hero from the very beginning.

11

HIS WORLD NEVER DIES

With his next Bond adventure, Daniel Craig will surpass Pierce Brosnan for third on the all-time list for most appearances as 007. It's quite an impressive achievement, considering the gaps between films have grown larger over the last 20 years.

Although it took some of the diehard fans (including myself) a substantial amount of time to grow accustomed to the blonde Bond, Craig has been great for the series. His version of the character, along with the elimination of sexist puns and better (although still not perfect) treatment of women, has brought the series successfully into the 21st century.

His next adventure, *Bond 25*, is scheduled to be released on April 8, 2020. It's original release was scheduled for Valentine's Day, which would have made for a great date, but I'll settle for taking my fiancée to catch the latest Bond film in April.[131]

---

[131] Umberto Gonzalez, "New Bond Film Pushed Back 2 Months from Valentine's Day 2020," *The Wrap*, Feb. 15, 2019, https://www.thewrap.com/james-bond-25-007-pushed-back-2020/.

But sooner rather than later, the series will be at a crossroads again in choosing the seventh actor to portray 007.

As of right now, the tabloids are more focused on the rumors of who could be the next 007. We're not going to discuss specifically who because there is nothing but speculation as of this publication. Bond producer Barbara Broccoli has publicly stated that she remains loyal to Craig and "cannot look beyond Daniel"[132] even though Craig has publicly stated that *Bond 25* will be his final go-around as 007.

He said the same thing after *Spectre,* so there's always a chance he could change his mind, but more than likely, a new face will represent Bond after 2020. Many people have argued that the new face should be entirely different -- either a different race or even sex.

For me, a woman playing James (Jane?) Bond would be too big of a change to the series. Obviously, the goal should be to continue bringing gender equality to 007, but it can be done without making a dramatic change to the main character.

While the series has expressed a willingness to adapt in this new century, most of the alterations have been slow and gradual. It seems unlikely the series would rebrand itself with Bond as a woman as early as the beginning of the next decade.

By all means, there should be more films made with women spies as main characters. But Bond is a story of an English male spy. Although many actors and actresses disagree with my

---

[132] "Bond producers not considering Richard Madden," *Female First,* Jan., 19, 2019, https://www.femalefirst.co.uk/movies/movie-news/bond-producers-considering-richard-madden-1180314.html.

take, Academy Award winning actress and Craig's wife, Rachel Weisz, concurs and explained it best to *Vanity Fair* in Feb. 2018:

"Why not create your own story rather than jumping onto the shoulders and being compared to all those other male predecessors?" Weisz said. "Women are really fascinating and interesting, and should get their own stories."[133]

This doesn't mean other improvements can't be made to the women in James Bond. For one, the series could begin phasing out the damsel in distress motif. It's been repeated so many times in the series, maybe it's time to finally see one of these strong, independent women save 007.

Well, actually, the audience has seen that; they probably just don't remember. In *From Russia with Love*, it's Tatiana (Daniela Bianchi) who shoots Rosa Klebb to help Bond avoid her shoe knife. Then in *Thunderball*, Domino shoots Largo in the back with a spear just as he begins to point a gun at 007.

In *On Her Majesty's Secret Service*, Bond escapes Blofeld's lair, but at a town fair in Lauterbrunnen, Switzerland, 007 finds himself surrounded. He stops trying to flee and sits on a park bench, practically admitting defeat and that his re-capture is imminent. Then, his future wife, Tracy di Vicenzo, happens to arrive, and she helps him escape.

---

[133] Yohana Desta, "Rachel Weisz Doesn't Want a Female James Bond: 'Women Should Get Their Own Stories,'" *Vanity Fair*, February 13, 2018, https://www.vanityfair.com/hollywood/2018/02/rachel-weisz-female-james-bond.

These scenes just need more dramatization and publicity. It's time the vulnerable Bond completely gives way to a female spy saving his life, thus showcasing the power of women.

Other people close to the series don't seem to be fans of Bond as a different race either. Three years ago in an interview with Paris Match Magazine, the late actor and former 007 Roger Moore seemed to reject the idea of a person from a different race playing Bond.

"Although James may have been played by a Scot, a Welshman and an Irishman, I think he should be 'English-English,'" Moore said. "Nevertheless it's an interesting idea... but unrealistic."[134]

It sounds like Moore is trying to argue that making Bond a different race is changing the original character from Fleming's novels too much. However, his comment comes across as racist, depending on how one interprets 'English-English,' which is a rather open-ended term.

Regardless, Moore was wrong. Portraying 007 as something other than white is completely different from making him a woman and should be heavily considered for *Bond 26* as long as it makes sense. Depicting Bond as black or Asian would help bring even more diversity to the series and potentially open up the series to a new audience.

When I say "as long as it make sense," the series shouldn't go out of its way to make Bond a different race -- it has to be an

---

[134] Roger Moore, Interview by Paris Match Magazine, 2015.

ethnic group that has a growing population in London or Great Britain.

The latest census is almost out of date, but according to the 2011 census, only 59.8 percent of London's population is white. There are more than one million Asian and black residents in the British city, as those groups combine to make up 31.7 percent of the London population.

It wouldn't make much sense to depict Bond as an Arab because only 1.3 percent of the London population is Arab.[135] But the new Bond could easily be from either black or Asian descent.

However, the race of the actor to play the next Bond is only the first of many questions the series will need to answer in the transition away from Craig.

With the blonde 007 in the last four films, the series has successfully rebooted itself. In *Spectre*, the series brought back Blofeld, and audiences embraced it.

But it won't be able to reboot itself again so soon. The next Bond is going to have to continue along the same trajectory Craig is on at the moment and hope the writing becomes a bit more original while moving away from relying so heavily upon evoking nostalgia.

Because at a certain point, films can't rely completely on nostalgia. Why continue to make new entries to the series if it's just going to be the same thing over and over again?

---

[135] "Ethnic Groups in London". *Census Update*. Office for National Statistics. 2011: 1. 11 December 2012. Retrieved 12 December 2011.

The answer to that question is because people are still going to see them, and thus, the series is still making money. But it's my belief that this won't continue if the audience feels they gain nothing from seeing the new film.

Going to watch the sea-version of *You Only Live Twice* ten years later (*The Spy Who Loved Me*) is one thing. But spending more than $15 (movie tickets are costly these days) to watch the series bring back moments from films you've already seen gets old after awhile.

One interesting element the series will offer fans in 2020 is the first reoccurring Bond girl in almost 60 years. The only other one in the series' history is Sylvia Trench, and she last appeared in *From Russia With Love*.

Léa Seydoux will be back as Dr. Madeleine Swann in *Bond 25*. Groundbreaking only begins to describe how important this is to the series.

Yes, the portrayal of women in the series has improved, but no woman has been important enough to return for a second film. Considering even ridiculous Sheriff Pepper received a second appearance in *The Man with the Golden Gun*, it's quite baffling the series didn't bring back one of its better Bond girls.

Despite the average fan mostly considering them mere sex objects, there were plenty of great Bond girls to choose from over the years to give a returning role. It's long overdue for one of them to receive more depth and character development.

The end of *Spectre* seemed to convey the feeling Bond was going to end up with Swann. They both expressed love for each other during the film, and while that's not necessarily unique to their relationship, this one felt different. The film's title theme song, "Writing's on the Wall" foreshadows this woman was going to be different in the opening credits.

> I've been here before
> But always hit the floor
> I've spent a lifetime running
> And I always get away
> But with you I'm feeling something
> That makes me want to stay
>
> *Chorus*
>
> If I risk it all
> Could you break my fall?
>
> How do I live? How do I breathe?
> When you're not here, I'm suffocating
> I want to feel love, run through my blood
> Tell me is this where I give it all up?
>
> For you, I have to risk it all
> 'Cause the writing's on the wall[136]

It wouldn't have surprised me if *Spectre* was Craig's last adventure and the series sent him riding off into the sunset in his Aston Martin with Swann. But her return, coupled with Craig's, suggests that Bond's relationships with women do matter.

Of course, maybe the series will provide the audience with a huge shock, and Swann becomes another sacrificial lamb, but

---

[136] Sam Smith. "Writing's on the Wall."

something tells me she's the woman Bond will consider retiring for again.

After 25 adventures, he deserves true love.

The Bond codename theory could help the series pull this off. If Craig's Bond is a different person than the next actor who plays him, then the next Bond can still "interact" with different women. This use of the codename theory could help the series continue to eliminate sexism and make the character less of a womanizer.

If I had my wish, Craig's 007 would indeed ride off into the sunset with Swann, and then the series picks up where it left off with a black 007 in *Bond 26*. The series can do this in a way that allows the audience to infer what they want -- a Bond-Swann marriage, the codename theory, etc. -- but without answering any real questions.

This potential transition could be tricky, but currently, the Bond series appears to be in excellent shape. The "Me Too" movement and liberal-minded millennials are a threat to the series, but as of now, it's not something that appears capable of killing it.

That is, as long as the series continues to adapt with the times. Continuing to modernize the character and moving Bond away from being a womanizer appears to be Craig's goal moving forward.

"I've been trying to do that gently for the past four movies, and I'll continue to do that," Craig said in April 2018 according to the Express.[137]

Another former Bond, Pierce Brosnan, has been much more forward thinking than Moore. He's called for black actors to play the role, but he doesn't anticipate the "Me Too" movement will directly impact the series.

"Well, I have no idea if the new films are going to address these social issues. I think Bond will continue in the same vein," he said in July 2018 according to The Indian Express.

"I would suspect so because men will continue to be men and women likewise. One hopes there will be more respect between the genders. You hope that good things come out of this 'Me Too' movement."[138]

No matter where the series goes next, it won't be able to please everyone. If Bond engages in meaningless sex, some viewers won't like it because it depicts women as unimportant sex objects. But should 007 exploit women to get the intel he needs, then there's a sect of the audience that will argue he's a cold-hearted bastard.

---

[137] George Simpson. "James Bond 25: 007 to become FEMINIST? Daniel Craig SPEAKS OUT," *The Express*, April 13, 2018, https://www.express.co.uk/entertainment/films/945614/James-Bond-25-Daniel-Craig-007-feminist-Me-Too-Times-Up-Danny-Boyle.

[138] PTI. "Pierce Brosnan says #MeToo will not affect James Bond films," *The Indian Express*. July 29, 2018, https://indianexpress.com/article/entertainment/hollywood/pierce-brosnan-james-bond-metoo-5281499/.

However, if the series makes the sex completely meaningful, suggesting 007 and the woman are in love, other critics will quibble that it isn't sincere or genuine. Eliminating sex altogether might work, but it's still an action series -- there almost always is a love interest in the genre.

One direction that could help is to continue showing women using their sex to exploit men. If Bond can use women, the women should be able to do the same to him.

In the last 20 years, Elektra King and Miranda Frost both slept with Bond to gain his trust and then backstabbed him. In *Quantum of Solace*, Camille Montes sleeps with Dominic Greene (Mathieu Amalric), the primary villain of the film, to get closer to General Medrano (Joaquin Cosio) and kill him.

Because of Bond's sexual history throughout the series, the film produces an ironically funny exchange between Bond and Montes when 007 asks her about her relationship with Greene.

> Bond: My sources tell me you're Bolivian Secret Service. Or used to be. That you infiltrated Greene's organization by having sex with him.
>
> Montes: [slight chuckling] That offends you?
>
> Bond: [with a smirk] No. Not in the slightest.[139]

If sex isn't going to be eliminated altogether, the series needs to emphasize gender equality, and the ability women possess to be just as conniving with the use of sex as men.

---

[139] *Quantum of Solace*. 2008.

Brosnan may have hit upon the right word -- respect. In today's environment, two people don't have to love each other to go to the bedroom together, but they should respect one another. When the series showcases sex as manipulation, it shouldn't be glorified as it was during the early stages of the series.

Furthermore, in modern times, men should always act respectfully towards women. Even if they are in the wrong (which, let's face it guys, is rare anyway), men should never hit a woman, which Bond did on several occasions in the 1960's and 1970's.

Those moments, along with other instances where the series takes advantage of women, displays sexist remarks, and conveys racist ideology, call into question whether fans should still cherish the original films.

It's a debate very similar to the one America had in regards to the "Baby, it's Cold Outside" Christmas song in Dec. 2018. The song possesses lyrics that some modern listeners have compared to date rape.

(Male lyrics are in parenthesis except where noted)

The neighbors might think (Baby, it's bad out there)
Say what's in this drink? (No cabs to be had out there)

I wish I knew how (Your eyes are like starlight now)
To break this spell (I'll take your hat, your hair looks swell)
(female: Why thank you)

I ought to say no, no, no sir (Mind if I move in closer?)
At least I'm gonna say that I tried (What's the sense of hurtin' my pride?)

I really can't stay (Baby, don't hold out)
Baby, it's cold outside[140]

Millennials are going back and scrutinizing a lot of cultural art from their parents and grandparents' generations. In most cases, millennials aren't wrong in their assessments, but it's up to the individual to decide if movies such as old Bond films or songs like "Baby, It's Cold Outside" are simply just products of their time or too vulgar and outdated to still enjoy.

Clearly, the series has some muddy water to navigate in the coming years. But through nearly six decades, nothing -- no villain nor social issue -- has been able to beat Bond. Like society, its evolution has been too slow moving at various points, and the series has sometimes suffered setbacks, but it eventually altered and persisted, carrying on many of its original traditions.

Maybe this comparison works for me because of the career path I chose, but the Bond series' evolution moving forward could somewhat mirror the transition of journalism in the 21st century. One day, neither may be recognizable to its original self, and that's not necessarily a bad thing.

There will likely come a day when people don't sit at the breakfast table and read a newspaper, but that doesn't mean there will be less journalism -- it's just going to be different. It will be on the internet, Twitter or whatever devices come out next.

---

[140] Lyrics by Frank Loesser, "Baby, It's Cold Outside," 1944.

The same goes for the Bond series. There may come a time when the 007 series no longer has the Bond girls or the sex element at all, leaving the series unrecognizable to a Baby Boomer. In one sense, breaking that tradition would be disappointing, but it could also mean producing an action series enjoyable to a wider demographic of people.

That change, though, is probably still years in the future, and as of today, there's no end to the series in sight.

As M stated in her Tennyson poem during *Skyfall*, "We are not now that strength which in old days moved earth and heaven, that which we are, we are. One equal temper of heroic hearts, made weak by time and fate, but strong in will. To strive, to seek, to find, and *not* to yield."[141]

For Mr. Bond, his world never dies.

---

[141] *Skyfall*. 2012.

ACKNOWLEDGEMENTS

To all of those who supported me through my first book venture, I thank you sincerely. I have the best support group. It has become too big to mention entirely by name, but I will personally thank as many as I can here.

First, I would like to thank my parents. My mother has been pushing me to write a book since I was young. I always thought maybe it would be something I could do when I was old and distinguished. But when I decided not to wait, her support never waivered.

Both my father and mother, Gary & Julie Holcomb, were the first to edit this book. They helped begin to shape the final direction of this story. More importantly, they heavily shaped the person I am today.

Secondly, thank you to my friend, Jake Hofstetter. He not only went with me to see my first Bond movie in theaters, he read my book before publishing and erased any self-doubts I possessed.

Next, I'd like to thank Andie Laps and the team at 100 Covers for designing a slam-dunk cover. Special thanks also to Rachael Cox for formatting my first book.

Also, thank you to my Uncle John for the advice he provided me on using James Bond in the subtitle. He took the time to ensure me I wouldn't run into any copyright trouble.

Thank you to Lisa Zelenak, who persuaded me to sign up for Self-Publishing School. I'm not easy to sway, especially when I have to fork over a lot of money, but Lisa convinced me to make the investment in myself, and I haven't regretted it once. Without Self-Publishing School, there's no way I could have self-published this book so quickly.

Through Self-Publishing School, I met Nick He, who began writing his own book at the same time as myself. Serving as my accountability partner in the course, Nick and I engaged in friendly weekly phone conversations, which inspired me to produce the best book I could.

I should also give a big shout-out to Gary Williams, Chandler Bolt and everyone else at Self-Publishing School that helped make my first book possible. My experience in the course couldn't have gone any better.

I'd also like to thank Phillip Lieb, who is one of many influential English teachers at Northern Highlands Regional High School. Lieb supplied me the photo of The History Gyre, which I learned about in his class during my junior year.

Lastly, thank you to my fiancée and the love of my life, Shannon. She unconditionally supports me, and that can't be easy with my freelance writer and sports journalist career. I'm usually the more even-keeled of the two of us, but it's hard to stay level-headed when I go periods without substantial work. Whenever I get nervous about my career though, she's my rock. Without her, this book wouldn't have been possible.

ABOUT THE AUTHOR

Dave Holcomb is a freelance writer, sports journalist and now, published author. He grew up in Pittsburgh, Pennsylvania and Allendale, New Jersey. Both places remain heavily influential upon his life.

Holcomb graduated with a dual major in Broadcast Journalism and English Textual Studies from Syracuse University in 2013. During his journalism career, he has covered the NFL, NHL, MLB, ACC sports, SEC football, fantasy sports and New Jersey high school sports.

He currently resides in Atlanta, where he manages Falcon Maven. Holcomb also writes for Yardbarker, Cox Media, Southern Pigskin and Rotowire. He lives with his fiancée, Shannon, and their two cats, Seth and Darwin.

He greatly appreciates the readers of his first book and would love their feedback. If you have the time, please provide a helpful review on Amazon.

Holcomb plans to write more books on subjects related to James Bond and/or other areas of his interest. Follow him on Twitter @dmholcomb.

DAVE HOLCOMB WILL RETURN

CPSIA information can be obtained
at www.ICGtesting.com
Printed in the USA
LVHW092243310720
662068LV00008B/228/J